WriteTraits®
STUDENT TRAITBOOK

Vicki Spandel • Jeff Hicks

GREAT SOURCE®
EDUCATION GROUP
A Houghton Mifflin Company

Vicki Spandel

Vicki Spandel was codirector of the original teacher team that developed the six-trait model and has designed instructional materials for all grade levels. She has written several books, including *Creating Writers—Linking Writing Assessment and Instruction* (Longman), and is a former language arts teacher, journalist, technical writer, consultant, and scoring director for dozens of state, county, and district writing assessments.

Jeff Hicks

Jeff Hicks has over 17 years of teaching experience in grades two through nine. Until recently, Jeff taught seventh- and eighth-grade English and math on a two-person teaching team, focusing on the reading/writing connection through six-trait writing activities. Currently, Jeff is a full-time writer and presenter.

Design/Production: Bill Westwood/Andy Cox

Illustration: Chris Vallo

Proofreading/Editorial: Erik Martin/Alex Culpepper, Judy Bernheim

Cover: Illustration by Claude Martinot Design

Package and Cover Design: Great Source/Kristen Davis

Printed in the United States of America

International Standard Book Number: 0-669-49041-5

4 5 6 7 8 9 10 - POO - 12 11 10 09 08 07 06

Contents

Unit 4: Word Choice

Unit 5: Sentence Fluency

Unit 6: Conventions

What's the Problem?

Read each sample carefully to identify the most obvious problem. There may be more than one, but one should stand out.

Sample 1

Cougars are highly interesting animals, but they can be dangerous. Cougars weigh from 150 to 180 pounds, on average, but can carry an amazing amount of weight. In fact, a cougar has been known to bring down a deer and then clear an eight-foot fence while carrying its prey in its mouth. Cougars can carry up to three times their own body weight, which would be like the average male human carrying 500 to 600 pounds. Cougars will attack humans, even when unprovoked, though such attacks are infrequent.

The MAIN problem with this sample seems to be

_____ the ORGANIZATION. The writer wanders off the main topic so much that this writing is very difficult to follow.

_____ the FLUENCY. The writer has interesting things to say, but begins almost every sentence the same way—it's monotonous!

Sample 2

Here is how to make a really good cake everyone will enjoy. First, start with a regular cake mix just like you would buy in the store. Then, instead of one or two eggs, put in three. It will make your cake moist. Instead of water, try adding buttermilk. Add some vanilla flavoring, too. Do not overmix the batter before you put it in the pan. Also, do not overbake the cake. This will dry it out. Make sure you do not frost it when it is still warm. This could make your frosting melt. Follow these directions and everyone will enjoy your cake.

The MAIN problem with this sample is

_____ the IDEAS. The piece really has no main idea, and it is hard to tell what the writer is talking about.

_____ the VOICE. This writer sounds so bored that it is hard for me not to be bored, too.

Warm-up Activity 2

Name That Revision Strategy

Identify the MAIN thing the writer did to revise.

Sample 1

Before

Everybody has a main characteristic. My brother Anthony forgets things. He forgets everything from his keys to his wallet. He is always losing school papers or forgetting to do an assignment. He forgets where he is supposed to be or when he is supposed to be there. He even forgets what he had for breakfast.

After

My brother Anthony is very forgetful. He forgets everything. If you asked him what he ate for breakfast this morning, he couldn't tell you. Looking for things such as his wallet, his keys, or his money is his favorite pastime. He has no idea where they are. Last night's assignment could be anywhere. He doesn't know where it is.

The MAIN thing this writer revised for was

_____ FLUENCY. The "After" version is much more fluent.

_____ WORD CHOICE. The "After" version uses colorful language, and the words are easier to understand.

Unit 1
Ideas

If you sleep too much, you may miss much of the day. On the other hand, if you sleep too little, you're likely to become tense and cranky. Balance is the key. Writing is like that, too. Of course, to know when you've hit that balance point, you need to think like a reader. Readers come to your text looking for ideas and information. Give them too little, and they leave feeling cheated. Overload them with more information than they can handle, and they're likely to doze off, missing the point you were hoping to make!

In this unit, you will practice achieving balance in your writing so that your readers will get the most out of your message. You'll learn about

◆ asking questions to narrow a topic

◆ using a prewriting strategy to collect ideas

◆ adding details to write clear, informative text

◆ cutting filler

name: .... date: ....

Will It Fit in My Backpack?

Sometimes it's a struggle to fit your binder, history book, math book, CD player, and lunch into your backpack. You "pack" a paper with details much the way you stuff your backpack with books and other belongings. The trick is to fit in everything you need without overpacking.

Imagine that your science teacher has just given you a research writing assignment. The topic you've selected is *plants,* which is a huge topic. Unless your paper turns into the world's biggest informational "backpack," you'll never fit in all the information that exists about plants. What's the solution? How about narrowing your topic to a manageable size?

Sharing an Example: Exploding Ants

In her book, *Exploding Ants: Amazing Facts About How Animals Adapt,* author and biology professor Joanne Settel, Ph.D., has narrowed her focus from biology in general, to interesting aspects of animal behavior: specifically, the strange eating

habits of some creatures, the ways they create places to live, and the ingenious ways some animals survive. Out of the thousands of examples she could have "packed" into her book, Dr. Settel has selected just a few to keep her topic manageable. This way, she informs her readers without weighing them down. Here's a sample passage about a liver fluke and how it actually gets to its home: a sheep's liver.

The tiny wormlike fluke is a *parasite* that spends different parts of its life inside the bodies of three different host animals: a snail, an ant, and a sheep. The fluke must get inside each host by being eaten. It uses its amazing reprogramming skills to get itself into the mouth of a hungry sheep.

Liver flukes actually begin their lives inside a snail. The snail starts things off when it eats some sheep dung filled with liver fluke eggs. Inside the snail, the eggs hatch, releasing thousands of tiny larvae (young flukes). As many as six thousand mucus-covered fluke larvae then gather together into a squirming ball. Eventually the snail ejects this grape-sized glob from its body.

The next step in the fluke's life cycle takes place when an ant feeds on the mucus ball. This brings the larvae into the ant's stomach, where they bore into the stomach wall. Most of the larvae remain here and grow into adult flukes.

Joanne Settel, Ph.D., *Exploding Ants: Amazing Facts About How Animals Adapt* (New York: Atheneum Books for Young Readers, 1999).

Write three things you learned about flukes from this passage:

1. _____

2. _____

3. _____

Which of the following comes closest to stating the main idea of Settel's passage?

_____ The world is full of interesting animals.

_____ The tiny fluke is a parasite with an unusual life cycle.

_____ Some animals are parasites and some are not.

From Probing Questions to Skinny Topics

One good way to narrow a huge topic is to ask some probing questions. What if you had a conversation with Dr. Settel to help her do just that? Work with a partner to see whether you can come up with four specific questions that Dr. Settel might have used to help narrow her topic. Write the responses Dr. Settel *might* have given to your questions. Remember, your goal is to end up with a narrowed topic.

Dr. Settel: _I'm a biology professor, and I want to write a book_ _about living things._

Question: _____

Dr. Settel: _____

Question: _____

Dr. Settel: _____

Question: _____

Dr. Settel: _____

Question: _____

Dr. Settel: _____

What Types of Questions?

Go back and look at each question you asked. How many of the following question words did you use? Circle each one.

Who   What   When   Where   Why   How   Which

Narrowing the Topic

Let's go back to the example research paper on plants from the introduction. If you were really going to write this paper, you'd first need to narrow your topic. Then create a conversation between yourself the **writer** and yourself the **questioner.** At the end of the conversation, you should be able to state your topic sentence. Your topic should easily "fit" into your research paper "backpack."

Writer: _I want to write a research paper on plants._

Questioner: _____

Writer: _____

Questioner: _____

Writer: _____

Questioner: _____

Writer: _____

Questioner: _____

My Topic Sentence:

_____

_____

_____

Does this topic now "fit" into my research paper "backpack"?

_____ Yes, it fits easily.

_____ It almost fits—just a bit more trimming needed.

_____ No way. I'm still writing a book on plants!

A Writer's Question

Imagine that you must write a research paper on plants, and you're going to do an Internet search to help you find information. How successful might that search be if you choose the general topic "plants"? How successful might it be if you used your new, narrowed topic?

name: .... date: ....

Setting the T-Table

Every once in a while, a great writing idea pops into your head, already narrowed down and crystal clear. More often, though, a fuzzy hint of an idea creeps into your mind, an idea that needs some help to take shape. Fuzzy hints sometimes blossom into full-blown ideas with the help of a prewriting tool such as a word list, an idea web, or a T-Table. A T-Table is a graphic organizer that you can use to gather details for your writing.

Sharing an Example: Men of Stone

Read the passage from the novel *Men of Stone* by Gayle Friesen. As you read, focus on the images the writer is creating and the reactions you have. In other words, what do you "see" and what do you "feel"? Write your thoughts in the T-Table. You don't have to write whole sentences, just notes to yourself.

The lines on her face were like earth that had gone too long without rain. It was a face that told a story, but not one I wanted to hear. She was a hundred years old if she was a day.

"Aunt Frieda would like to come for a visit" was the way Mom had opened the family conference a week ago.

"Aunt who?" my sisters and I asked simultaneously.

"You know," Mom insisted.

No we didn't.

"Your father's aunt . . . your great-aunt," Mom prodded. "She's asked if she could come and spend some time with us."

"Why?" Again, the question was more or less unanimous. Unusual too, since we hardly ever agreed on anything.

Mom shrugged and poured another cup of coffee. Her chin had twitched the way it did when something was bugging her. "She said she was old."

"That's her reason?" I asked.

"I guess, I really don't know her that well. I haven't even seen her since the um, funeral."

The um-funeral. My dad. He died ten years ago. I was five.

Gayle Friesen, *Men of Stone* (Tonawanda, New York: Kids Can Press, Ltd., 2000), pp. 9–10.

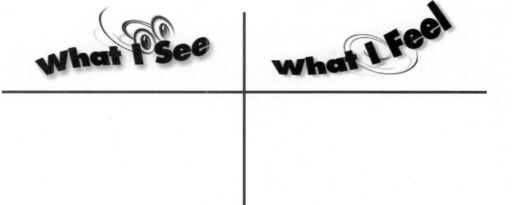

A Nonfiction Example: Undaunted Courage

On page 14, you will read some informational writing from Stephen E. Ambrose's book, *Undaunted Courage.* Use the T-Table that goes with it and follow the same procedure you used with the first passage. Though this is informational writing, pay attention to what you see and feel. What you find may be very different from what you noticed in the passage from the novel.

Since the birth of civilization, there had been almost no changes in commerce or transportation. Americans lived in a free and democratic society, the first in the world since ancient Greece, a society that read Shakespeare and had produced

George Washington and Thomas Jefferson, but a society whose technology was barely advanced over that of the Greeks. The Americans of 1801 had more gadgets, better weapons, a superior knowledge of geography, and other advantages over the ancients, but they could not move goods or themselves or information by land or water any faster than had the Greeks and Romans. . . .

But only sixty years later, when Abraham Lincoln took the Oath of Office as the sixteenth president of the United States, Americans could move bulky items in great quantity farther in an hour than Americans of 1801 could do in a day, whether by land (twenty-five miles per hour on railroads) or water (ten miles an hour upstream on a steamboat). This great leap forward in transportation—a factor of twenty or more—in so short a space of time must be reckoned as the greatest and most unexpected revolution of all—except for another technological revolution, the transmitting of information. In Jefferson's day, it took six weeks to move information from the Mississippi River to Washington, D.C. In Lincoln's, information moved over the same route by telegraph all but instantaneously.

Stephen E. Ambrose, *Undaunted Courage: Meriwether Lewis, Thomas Jefferson, and the Opening of the American West* (New York: Touchstone, 1996), pp. 53–54.

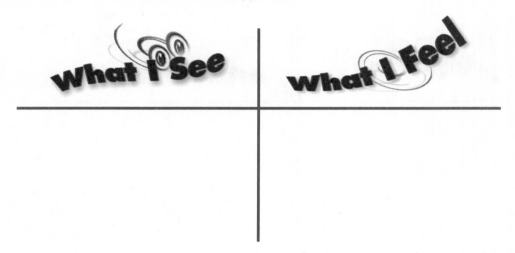

Quick Share

Meet with a partner to compare T-Tables. Did you each notice the same things? Which side was easier to fill in? Feel free to add anything to your table based on your discussion.

Connecting to the Traits

Whether it is in a novel or an informational piece, writing that creates clear pictures for readers is strong in the trait of ideas. If you were able to fill in the "What I See" side of both T-Tables, both writers must have selected and included the right details, examples, and information. If you were able to fill in the "What I Feel" side of both T-Tables, both writers knew their topics well, were committed to their topics, and created images that produced personal reactions.

Your Turn to T-Off

Now it's time to use a T-Table as a prewriting tool. First, choose a writing topic. (Look in your writing folder for an idea.) Using the T-Table that follows, write three to five things on each side that you definitely want your readers to notice in your writing. Don't create sentences yet—just short notes. If you choose an informational topic, you'll definitely want your readers to feel the confidence that comes from your knowledge of the topic.

A Writer's Question

How could you use a T-Table as an after-writing activity to help guide your revision?

No Doubt About It

I'll never forget that one time in that place. We were all there, and it was great!

There is no doubt about who's doing all the work with this writing—the reader! Your reader's brain desperately wants to make sense of the words and ideas, but it's spinning with questions: Who is the narrator? Why was this time so unforgettable? Where is "that place"? What was so great about it? With its foggy language and nonexistent details, this writing cannot stand alone. Revision is necessary to turn this foggy text into clear, detailed writing.

Sharing an Example: A Woolly Mammoth Journey

Below is a passage from a fictional story by Debbie S. Miller about a family of woolly mammoths on a cross-country trek. The author has created this story to show what the world was like for these long-extinct creatures 10,000 years ago. Notice how she includes physical and behavioral details about the mammoths as she describes the action of the moment.

The young bulls of the family like to explore. One afternoon Wise One's curious son follows another bold bull. They playfully butt heads, click their tusks, and coil their trunks together. Bold One is adventurous. He trots off along the riverbank, with Curious One trailing him. As they move up the river, the cutbanks grow higher and steeper. Bold One follows the edge of the river bluff, looking for an easy route down to the water.

Suddenly, a huge wedge of ground collapses beneath Bold One. He tumbles down the steep slope in a landslide of dirt and boulders. Curious One can no longer see Bold One and trumpets loudly in fright.

Debbie S. Miller, *A Woolly Mammoth Journey* (Boston: Little, Brown and Company, 2001).

Stand-Alone Writing

Can this passage stand alone? Let's analyze it to find out. Complete the chart with specific words or phrases from the passage that helped you picture the mammoths in action along the riverbank.

Words or Phrases	
Bold One	
Curious One	
Setting	
Mammoth behavior	

Based on your analysis, does the author create a clear picture of two adventurous mammoth bulls getting themselves into trouble?

_____ Yes   _____ No

Would you call this a sample of writing that stands alone?

_____ Definitely—nothing foggy here!

_____ *Almost*—though some things need explaining.

_____ Not at all—it's too hard to follow without the author right here to explain it.

Share and Compare

Meet with a partner or small group to compare the words and phrases on your charts. Feel free to add anything you may have missed. Then, compare your analyses. Can this piece stand alone? What do you think? What does your partner think?

Break It Down

What if the author had written the following sentences instead of the passage above?

Some mammoths are adventurous and bold. This leads to trouble.

What's missing from this version? Put a check by any of the following elements that you think are lacking.

- Clear, accurate word choice _____
- Sensory language and details _____
- Setting or character details _____
- Evidence of research or experience _____

You probably checked most items on the list. The items on the list are what writers use to create clear, detailed writing that stands alone. The "revised," shortened version doesn't even come close to doing that. In this next part, we'll start with a piece of writing that does not stand alone, and you can enhance it with some stronger details.

Leave No Doubt in Your Readers' Minds!

Here's a piece of foggy writing for you to rescue. Read it through one time to get a feel for it. Then, close your eyes. Can you picture what the author is writing about? Do the words stand alone? Read it again with a pencil or pen in your hand. Think back to the checklist under "Break It Down." Circle any words that need replacing, and make notes to yourself in the margins about details or

descriptions that need to be added. Then, rescue the writing by revising it according to your notes. Make it clear enough to stand alone.

Before (Foggy and in need of serious help):

This year on the Fourth of July, the neighbors were really out of control. They had a lot more fireworks than last year. They had a bunch that were really noisy and some that were really bright. I felt nervous all night. I knew something bad would happen.

After (Focused, strong, and able to stand alone):

_____

_____

_____

_____

_____

_____

_____

_____

A Writer's Question

What exactly did you do in your revision to improve the foggy writing? Describe at least three kinds of changes you made to help focus the writing.

_____

_____

_____

Just Right

Ask anyone who's had that second (or third) piece of chocolate cake: Too much of a good thing can be as bad as too little. Overcrowding your writing with unneeded information, details, or descriptions (filler) distracts and tires readers just as much as requiring them to fill in missing information. If you find filler in your writing, put the writing away for a couple of hours, a day, or even a week. Come back to it later, and you'll see your writing with a fresher perspective.

Sharing an Example: Artemis Fowl

Here's a short passage, focusing on the title character, from Eoin Colfer's futuristic fantasy tale, *Artemis Fowl.* Read it carefully, noticing what the author wants you to know about Artemis. Does he avoid overloading you with filler?

After eighteen solid hours of sleep and a light continental breakfast, Artemis climbed to the study that he had inherited from his father. It was a traditional enough room—dark oak and floor-to-ceiling shelving—but Artemis had jammed it

name: .... date: ....

with the latest computer technology. A series of networked AppleMacs whirred from various corners of the room. One was running CNN's Web site through a DAT projector, throwing oversized current-affairs images against the back wall.

Butler was there already, firing up the hard drives.

"Shut them all down, except the Book. I need quiet for this."

The manservant started. The CNN site had been running for almost a year. Artemis was convinced that news of his father's rescue would come from there. Shutting it down meant that he was finally letting go.

"All of them?"

Artemis glanced at the back wall for a moment. "Yes," he said finally. "All of them."

Butler took the liberty of patting his employer gently on the shoulder, just once, before returning to work. Artemis cracked his knuckles. Time to do what he did best—plot dastardly acts.

Eoin Colfer, *Artemis Fowl* (New York: Hyperion Books for Children, 2001), pp. 29–30.

What Did You Find Out?

In this passage, the author is beginning to create a picture of Artemis and his world. In the box below, write at least five details about Artemis or the world in which he lives. If you think the author has left in some filler, write that information outside the box.

Artemis and His World

_____

_____

_____

_____

_____

_____

What If?

What if while trying to shed light on Artemis and his world, the author had loaded his text with filler? Instead of getting a clear picture of Artemis, you might have felt so confused and annoyed that you lost interest in the book altogether. Getting rid of filler is one important step in good revision. Read the following sample, and notice the details that were cut.

After eighteen solid hours of sleep and a light continental breakfast ~~of two apple pastries and fresh squeezed orange juice~~, Artemis climbed ~~the twenty-two steps of the iron spiral staircase~~ to the study that he had inherited from his father. It was a traditional enough room—dark oak and floor-to-ceiling shelving, ~~four walls, lights, plush brown carpeting~~—but Artemis had jammed it with the latest computer technology. A series of networked AppleMacs ~~connected by what seemed like miles of dark gray cable and phone lines~~ whirred from various corners of the room. One was running CNN's Web site through a DAT projector, throwing oversized current-affairs images against the back wall, ~~which unlike the other walls was not covered in book shelves, framed art, or school pictures of Artemis~~.

Do you agree that the added filler resulted in information overload?

_____ Yes! I would have crossed it out, too.

_____ Mostly, though I liked some of these extra details.

_____ Not at all! I would leave in every one of these details and add a whole bunch more to make sure that I had plenty of detail for readers who enjoy words.

Crossing Out Filler

Now it's your turn to clear out the distractions. With a pen or pencil in hand, read the following passage, looking closely for information that is just taking up space. When you spot it, draw a line through it. To make sure you've found all the filler, you may want to read the passage a second time.

A War Zone

The people in our neighborhood must have been feeling especially patriotic this year because I've never seen or heard so many fireworks on the Fourth of July. Once the sun set, it sounded like a war zone up and down our street. We usually get a special permit from the city police to block off our street from around 4:00 in the afternoon until about 11:00 P.M. The woman across the street is the one who takes care of the permit. She knows who to call. She is a very civic-minded person, always getting involved in local and neighborhood issues. There are always committee meetings at her house. The other neighbor across the street is the one who organizes the barbecue and food. This year my mom made a macaroni salad and an apple cake. Both were really good. My dad doesn't believe in spending very much for fireworks because we have a couple neighbors who always buy a huge arsenal of just about everything that sparks, whistles, flames, and booms. Last year, the little boy who lives across the street spent the whole day indoors because the noise freaked him out. This year he announced, "I'm four. I like fireworks now."

Share and Compare

Take turns sharing your revised versions with a partner. Were you able to find and eliminate the filler? Did you cross out the same parts? Be willing to discuss why you decided to remove the lines you did, especially if there are any differences of opinion. After you talk, it's OK to make changes based on your discussions.

A Writer's Question

How do you know which details to cut and which ones to keep in a piece of writing? What sort of rules or personal system do you use?

Organization

Imagine that someone took all the letters on this page, stirred them up like ingredients in a big pot of soup, and then dumped them back on the page. Could you sort the letters and recreate these same sentences again? You probably could reassemble some words or maybe even some sentences, but you'd have a tough time reassembling this original message. Without the right organization, even the most powerful message is unlikely to reach the reader in the way the writer intended. Readers depend on organization to make sense of what a writer is saying.

This unit will help you practice some organizational strategies to ensure that your message gets through. You will learn about

◆ eight organizational patterns

◆ selecting the appropriate organizational pattern for the topic and purpose

◆ using transitions to connect ideas

◆ putting together all the organizational pieces

name: .... date: ....

Looking for a Pattern

In every police drama, detectives who are hot on the trail of a criminal look carefully at all the clues left behind, trying to find a *pattern* that will help them solve the case. Writers are big on patterns, too. Writers select organizational patterns to fit their topic and purpose—and not every pattern goes well with every topic. A description of a Gila monster calls for one kind of organization, and a recipe for scones calls for another. Choosing wisely makes all the difference because great ideas, compelling voice, and powerful word choice may go unnoticed if readers have to put all their energy into just following the information. In this lesson, you'll become familiar with five organizational patterns and then choose the one that you think is a good match for a piece of writing you will create.

A Palette of Patterns

Read the following ways to organize writing. Are any patterns familiar? Put a check mark next to each pattern that you have used before.

_____ **Chronological (Time) Order** You can arrange details in the order in which they happened (first, second, then, next, later, and so on). Autobiographical and biographical essays are almost always organized chronologically, as are science and history reports.

_____ **Order of Location (Spatial)** You can arrange details in the order in which they are located (above, below, beneath, and so on). Descriptions, observational reports, and certain explanations (such as giving directions) are organized spatially.

_____ **Order of Importance** You can arrange details from the most important to the least—or from the least important to the most. Persuasive essays, news stories, and most expository essays are organized by order of importance.

_____ **Cause and Effect** You can begin with a general statement giving the cause of a problem and then add a number of specific effects. Essays that explore or analyze problems (often based on current events) are organized in this way. **Note:** The problem and solution method is closely related to the cause and effect method of organization. You state a problem and explore possible solutions.

_____ **Comparison** You can develop two or more subjects by showing how they are alike and how they are different.

Patrick Sebranek, Dave Kemper, Verne Meyer, *Write Source 2000* (Wilmington, MA: Great Source Education Group, 1999), p. 60.

Pick a Pattern, Please

Here are three short writing samples, each using one of the organizational patterns you just read about. As you read each sample, decide which pattern the author used. You may find it helpful to try an active reading strategy: circle important words or phrases that are clues to the pattern. After you've found the pattern, write its name on the line.

Sample 1

Summer thunder and lightning storms can do more than start forest fires. They can even put a swimming pool out of business, at least temporarily. Guests at the Lazy River Inn woke up this morning to discover that last night's electrical storm had knocked out the pump on the resort's largest pool. According to a resort spokesperson, this has

happened before but not in the middle of a heat wave. The temperature was already in the upper eighties as guests began lining up just before 10 a.m., the pool's usual opening time. A wave of disappointment swept over the swimsuit-clad crowd as the bad news was announced over the PA system.

Organizational Pattern _____

Sample 2

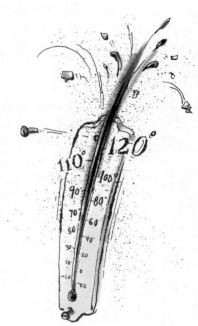

We had hot summers in eastern Nebraska where I was born. Often the temperature rose to well over 100° Fahrenheit, with high humidity to match. Our clothes would become so damp from a walk or bike ride that we'd have to change twice a day just to keep ourselves from sticking to the furniture. We never could get enough of the pool! Now we live in Arizona, where summer temperatures are even hotter, yet we seldom complain. Perhaps that's because more buildings are air-conditioned, or it may be the lack of humidity. Arizona has a far drier climate than Nebraska, winter or summer.

Organizational Pattern _____

Sample 3

My dad is always telling stories about the unusual things he spots on his evening run. This evening I decided to tag along—just to see what the big deal was. About a mile and a half west of our house, just over a steep hill, we were passed by a speeding biker carrying a small white poodle in her red backpack. Its ears were blowing back in the wind. Two blocks later, we came to a red brick house with a huge front lawn, stretching out like an inviting carpet. On the edge of a pond flanked by rocks, a raccoon was happily

catching goldfish—and eating them. The street has a wide bike lane on both sides and a sidewalk on the left. Right in the middle of the sidewalk I spotted it: a blue and white running shoe with the lace missing. I couldn't help wondering what the next turn in the road would bring.

Organizational Pattern _____

Following a Pattern

Now that you are becoming familiar with organizational patterns, select one of the five patterns and write a paragraph (eight or more sentences). The topic is up to you.

_____

_____

_____

_____

_____

_____

_____

_____

_____

A Writer's Question

Many writers feel most comfortable with the *Chronological Order* pattern. Why do you think this is? What problems could a writer encounter if he or she were comfortable with only one pattern?

name: .... date: ....

Finding the Perfect Match

Remember that old memory game with playing cards? You place all the cards face down on a table, and when it's your turn, you flip over two cards, trying for a match. At first, you're just guessing, but the point is to test your visual memory. Writers play a matching game as well, selecting an organizational pattern that fits the message. If the match is a good one, the organizational pattern can make the message both interesting and easy to process.

Eight Eligible Candidates

In Lesson 5, you reviewed five commonly used organizational patterns. For this activity, you'll see three more. Read the descriptions carefully, and put a check next to each one you have used.

Five familiar friends . . .

_____ **Chronological (Time) Order** You can arrange details in the order in which they happened (first, second, then, next, later, and so on). Autobiographical and biographical essays are almost always organized chronologically, as are science and history reports.

_____ **Order of Location (Spatial)** You can arrange details in the order in which they are located (above, below, beneath, and so on.) Descriptions, observational reports, and certain explanations (such as giving directions) are organized spatially.

_____ **Order of Importance** You can arrange details from the most important to the least—or from the least important to the most. Persuasive essays, news stories, and most expository essays are organized by order of importance.

_____ **Cause and Effect** You can begin with a general statement giving the cause of a problem and then add a number of specific effects. Essays that explore or analyze problems (often based on current events) are organized in this way. **Note:** The problem-and-solution method is closely related to the cause-and-effect method of organization. You state a problem and explore possible solutions.

_____ **Comparison** You can develop two or more subjects by showing how they are alike and how they are different.

Patrick Sebranek, Dave Kemper, Verne Meyer, *Write Source 2000* (Wilmington, MA: Great Source Education Group, 1999), p. 60.

And three new ones . . .

_____ **Point and Counterpoint** This is often used to make persuasive writing more convincing. Both sides of an argument are presented. This way the writer anticipates the opposing side's counterpoints.

_____ **Main Events** This pattern works well for biographies, summaries, and other forms of writing. A biography or summary might include only the most important events or information rather than trying to tell everything.

_____ **Step-by-Step** This is very appropriate for directions, lab procedures in science, and so on—any time you need to explain to your readers how to do something.

Write a Match for It

Seven writing tasks are listed. Read each task carefully, and write the purpose for each task. Consider which pattern will involve the reader and which pattern will make the message clear. Write your answers in the blank spaces.

Writing Tasks

1. A detailed account for a car owner's manual on how to change a flat tire

   Organizational Pattern _____

2. An article for the school newspaper about the new principal

   Organizational Pattern _____

3. An editorial in favor of changing the school's mascot and team names

   Organizational Pattern _____

4. A series of journal entries about your summer trip to Washington, D.C.

   Organizational Pattern _____

5. An aerial description of Mount St. Helens after your helicopter tour of the site

   Organizational Pattern _____

6. An editorial analyzing which of two films should win an award

   Organizational Pattern _____

7. A voter's pamphlet explaining why you should vote for a new sales tax

   Organizational Pattern _____

Share and Compare

Meet with a partner to share your choices for each of the seven writing tasks. Be ready to explain the reasons behind your choices. Is it possible for you and your partner to have made different choices and yet both be right? Why or why not?

Pattern Practice

Write a short paragraph (at least eight sentences) on the general topic "games." Choose an organizational pattern for your topic. Before you write, ask yourself: *What is my main message? Which organizational pattern will best suit my writing purpose?*

My message: _____

Organizational pattern I selected: _____

_____

_____

_____

_____

_____

_____

_____

_____

_____

_____

_____

A Writer's Question

Suppose that you use one organizational pattern for a piece of writing, but as you write more, another pattern suddenly seems more appropriate. What's probably going on with your writing? Should you rewrite using the more appropriate organizational pattern? Why or why not?

Lesson 7

Clear Connections

Have you ever been disconnected from a telephone conversation? The line goes dead, and then you hear static or nothing at all. If you stay disconnected long enough, you probably won't remember why you called in the first place. Readers can get "disconnected" from your writing if you don't link ideas together clearly. In writing, good connections are called *transitions*. Clear, strong transitions enhance a reader's understanding of how each small idea, sentence, and paragraph connects to the writer's main idea.

Sharing an Example: Red Scarf Girl

Author Ji Li Jiang's memoir, *Red Scarf Girl,* tells about growing up in China during Mao Ze-dong's Cultural Revolution. Her family was shunned by neighbors and former friends and lived in constant fear of harassment and arrest. Read the following passage about Ji Li's grandmother, who came to live with them to escape trouble. The transition words and phrases have been highlighted for you. As you read, notice how these highlighted words guide you.

I remembered coming home from kindergarten and showing Grandma the songs and dances we had learned. Grandma sat before us with her knitting, nodding her head in time to the music. Sometimes we insisted that she sing with us, and she would join in with an unsteady pitch and heavy Tianjin accent, wagging her head and moving her arms just as we did.

When we tired of singing, we would pester Grandma to show us her feet. When she was young it was the custom to tightly bind girls' feet in bandages to make them as small as possible—sometimes as small as three inches long. This was considered the height of a woman's beauty. Grandma's feet were half bound, and when she was only seven she fought to have them released. As a result her feet were smaller than natural feet but larger than bound ones. We loved to touch them and play with them. If she refused to let us, we would tickle her until she panted with laughter.

All my friends loved coming to our home because she was so friendly. She had lived in our alley for over thirty years without a single disagreement with any of the neighbors. Everyone loved her and respected her.

Ji Li Jiang. *Red Scarf Girl: A Memoir of the Cultural Revolution* (New York: Harper Trophy, 1997), pp. 121–122.

Words That Connect

The author Ji Li Jiang has used a variety of transitions. Compare Ji Li Jiang's transitions with the more inclusive list of transitions below. The words and phrases have been grouped based on purpose, showing the many ways transitions can help readers stay connected to a writer's message.

Transitions

Words that can be used to **show location:**

above	behind	by	near	throughout
across	below	down	off	to the right
against	beneath	in back of	onto	under
along	beside	in front of	on top of	
among	between	inside	outside	
around	beyond	into	over	

Words that can be used to **show time:**

while	first	meanwhile	soon	then
after	second	today	later	next

at	third	tomorrow	afterward	as soon as
before	now	next week	immediately	when
during	until	yesterday	finally	suddenly

Words that can be used to **compare** two things:

| likewise | as | while | in the same way |
| like | also | similarly | |

Words that can be used to **contrast** two things (show differences between them):

| but | still | although | on the other hand |
| however | yet | otherwise | even though |

Patrick Sebranek, Dave Kemper, Verne Meyer. *Write Source 2000* (Wilmington, MA: Great Source Education Group, 1999), p. 106.

A Little Practice

Here's a short passage from *Orvis,* a science fiction novel by H. M. Hoover. With a pencil in hand (and the list of transitional words and phrases to refer to), carefully read the passage. As you read, underline any transitions. Underline *any* words or phrases that help you connect one idea to another.

With Orvis's instructions and the glass shard for a knife, they managed. More than an hour passed before the pheasants were ready to be spitted. By that time both birds and children looked much the worse for wear.

Leaving Orvis to turn the spit, they went to wash in the creek. She scrubbed her hands with sand until they tingled but her fingers still smelled of raw poultry.

"Is this a character-building experience?" Thaddeus was kneeling on a rock, cleaning his nails with a split twig. "When we have to do something hard in physical therapy or gym, the coach says it's 'character-building.'"

H. M. Hoover, *Orvis* (New York: Starscape Books, 1987), p. 126.

Share and Compare

Before sharing with the class, meet with a partner and share your work. Closely compare your underlined transitions, and discuss any differences between your marks and your partner's.

Creating a Strong Connection

Read the next piece of writing carefully. If you find a transition that isn't right or doesn't fit, replace it with a stronger one or cross it out. If you see a place where a transition is needed, insert a helpful word or phrase. Refer to the list from pages 34–35 to help you find the word or phrase that will clearly connect the ideas. Reword any sentences as needed so that all transitions read smoothly.

Our county fair has this really strange event that combines a couple of traditional fair activities. For this reason, it's known as the pig and Ford races. Beyond this event, they release a whole bunch of greased pigs as the contestants are standing by their vehicles—old hand-cranked Ford flatbed trucks. Later, the starter fires his gun, so the contestants run around and try to grab hold of one of the pigs. In the same way, anyone who can catch a pig carries it to his or her truck before trying to crank-start the truck. To repeat, when the trucks are running, drivers have to guide them beneath the arena to the finish line. The winner afterward gets to keep the pig.

A Writer's Question

Missing or weak transitions definitely can be a problem. But what about transition overload? Can a writer go too far and put in so many linking words that it's overwhelming for the reader?

name: .... date: ....

Creating the Total Package

By now you might be thinking, "Hey, real writers spend their time writing, not just practicing all these separate parts. When do I get to work on the total writing package?" How about right now? Use your writing skills to put all the organizational components together. Remember, you're in control. You get to decide how to begin, where to go next, how to connect, and how to wrap it up.

A Smart Shopper

Try to imagine yourself at an *information* shopping mall, pushing a shopping cart labeled "MFT" (My Focused Topic). You're a smart shopper, so you don't want to pass up any "bargains," but you don't want to end up with a cart that's so full you can't push it. You enter the store called "Earth" and find the section on "Earthquakes." All the following facts and details are available. Think of this information as background research for a paragraph you will write about earthquakes. Which facts and details will you put into your writer's MFT cart? As you read, put a star next to the items you want,

and put an X next to the items you're leaving on the shelf because they are too general or uninteresting or don't match well with your other items. WARNING: If you pick up more than half the items on this shelf, you'll make your writing task difficult!

_____ **1.** The earth is formed of several layers.

_____ **2.** An earthquake is the often severe vibration of the surface of the earth that comes after some kind of energy release in the earth's crust—volcanic eruptions, human-made explosions, the "plates" that make up the outer layers sliding over or under one another.

_____ **3.** Faults are breaks in the earth's crust.

_____ **4.** Earthquakes often recur along faults.

_____ **5.** Earthquakes can be very destructive.

_____ **6.** Landslides caused by earthquakes are often more destructive than the earthquakes themselves.

_____ **7.** Earthquakes happen in many parts of the world.

_____ **8.** If an earthquake originates below the ocean's surface, it can create huge waves called tsunamis.

_____ **9.** Seismographs are instruments that detect, record, and measure vibrations caused by earthquakes.

_____ **10.** Information from seismographs is often broadcast on your local weather channel.

_____ **11.** The Richter scale measures the magnitude of earthquakes. A magnitude of 2.0 is the smallest quake usually detected by people; magnitudes of 6.0 or more are considered major.

_____ **12.** The Richter scale is named after Dr. Charles F. Richter of the California Institute of Technology.

_____ **13.** The U.S. Geological Survey does research on the likelihood of future earthquakes.

_____ **14.** The largest earthquake of the twentieth century measured 9.50 and occurred off the coast of Chile in 1960.

_____ **15.** A tsunami from the Chile earthquake hit Hawaii, killing 61 people.

___ **16.** If you are inside a building during an earthquake, it is usually safer to stay inside and take cover underneath something sturdy, like a desk.

___ **17.** During an earthquake, many people are injured by falling debris from buildings and from downed electrical lines.

___ **18.** California, Nevada, Idaho, Montana, Washington, Hawaii, Arkansas, Missouri, and Alaska have each had one or more earthquakes of magnitude 7.0 or higher in the last 200 years.

___ **19.** Earthquakes in 1811 and 1812, near the border of Arkansas and Missouri, changed the course of the Mississippi River and even forced the river to flow backward for several hours.

___ **20.** You should avoid standing near windows, mirrors, and heavy furniture such as bookshelves, during an earthquake.

What's in Your MFT Cart?

Take a close look at the items you put into your MFT shopping cart. How did you do?

___ I overloaded. I need to take some items out.

___ I shopped too fast—I don't have enough items.

___ I have just enough information with no overload.

Bringing It into Focus

Look at all the items you chose. Do they go together? Is there a common theme? What is one main idea or point you wish to make about earthquakes? If some items don't fit, this is a good time to toss them out. Write your main idea or message here.

_____

_____

What's the Pattern?

Given your message, what type of organizational pattern would be best for your topic? Look back to Lesson 6 to refresh your memory about different organizational patterns. Write your choice here.

_____

Off to a Hot Start

Your lead needs to tantalize those readers who didn't know how interesting earthquakes could be. Dip into your cart one more time and find the one detail that jumps out as a great place to start. Use it to write one possible lead here.

_____

_____

Keep the Energy Flowing

Use the energy from your lead to help you flow right into the rest of your piece. Start with the lead you just wrote or write a new one. As you sequence your details, remember the organizational pattern you selected. Be sure to wrap up with a strong conclusion.

_____

_____

_____

_____

A Writer's Question

How does focusing on organization— lead, organizational pattern, transitions, conclusion—end up strengthening your ideas? What's the connection between organization and ideas?

Unit 3 Voice

Have you ever eaten something with no taste whatsoever? "Why bother eating it?" you might ask. Suppose someone said, "Look, this stuff is really good for you. It's jam-packed with vitamins! It's bursting with minerals!" Do you think you'd like the food any better? Face it; without flavor, food is unappealing, no matter how many other good things we can say about it. Writing is a lot like that. We can put the best information available in front of readers, but if we haven't flavored it with some voice, they probably won't take more than a nibble and would ask, "Why bother reading it?"

In this unit, you'll learn some strategies for flavoring your writing. You'll learn about

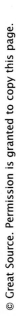

- ◆ defining personal voice
- ◆ using voice in informational writing
- ◆ matching voice to audience
- ◆ revising to add voice

name: ....   date: ....

A Defining Moment

In this exciting lesson, your entire future will be defined by the path you choose and by how courageously you act in the face of danger. Well, that's a *slight* exaggeration. But even though your destiny may not hang in the balance, this defining moment is still important. It's all about creating a personal definition of voice as it relates to writing. Why does voice matter so much? Because your concept of voice can help you evaluate the strengths and weaknesses of your writing, whether you're working on a narrative essay, a technical report, an imaginative story, or poetry. You'll begin by listening to a sampling of writers' voices and deciding which ones appeal to readers and why. Then you will reach your defining moment: your personal definition of voice.

Three to Get Ready

Read each of these sample passages carefully—more than once, in fact—to make sure you don't miss anything. *See* the words, *picture* the ideas, and *hear* the voice coming through. Use the scale following each passage to assess the *amount* of voice you heard. Then, write down words that describe each writer's voice.

Voice 1

Longstreet felt a depression so profound it deadened him. Gazing back on that black hill above Gettysburg, that high lighted hill already speckled with fires among the gravestones, he smelled disaster like distant rain.

It was Longstreet's curse to see the thing clearly. He was a brilliant man who was slow in speech and slow to move and silent-faced as stone. He had not the power to convince. He sat on the horse, turning his mind away, willing it away as a gun barrel swivels, and then he thought of his children, powerless to stop that vision. It blossomed: a black picture. She stood in the doorway: *the boy is dead.* She didn't even say his name. She didn't even cry.

Longstreet took a long deep breath. In the winter the fever had come to Richmond. In a week they were dead. All within a week, all three. He saw the sweet faces: moment of enormous pain. The thing had pushed him out of his mind, insane, but no one knew it.

Michael Shaara, *The Killer Angels* (New York: Ballantine Books, 1974), pp. 126–127.

BARELY ANY VOICE. 1 2 3 4 5 6 STRONG, CLEAR VOICE!

Words that describe this voice: _____

_____

Voice 2

Grandpa asked me whether I noticed anything different about the place, directing my attention to the eastern fence line. We hadn't been here for almost six months, and we'd barely gotten out of the car. I looked to Grandma for help, but she just smiled and looked away. My mom, dad, and sister were taking bags into the house, so I was on my own. "You look a bit older," I thought but I didn't say it. He loved doing things like this to me. He was always testing my "powers of observation," as he called them. He had told me in a phone call that my Uncle John had trimmed the big tree that could be seen from where we were standing. I knew that wouldn't count. Grandma had more flowerpots on the deck, but she always did. I knew that wouldn't count either. I thought hard about the porch swing. Was that there the last time we were here? And then I got it, but I got it too late. My sister came out onto the deck and shouted, "Hey, the old horse barn is gone!"

BARELY ANY VOICE. **1 2 3 4 5 6** STRONG, CLEAR VOICE!

Words that describe this voice: _____

_____

Voice 3

"Two thousand one hundred and sixty adventures. Two thousand one hundred and sixty opportunities to become whatever you want to become. This is what you've been waiting six years for. This is the day it begins."

She wishes she had a camera.

She looks at the clock above the door. She acts surprised. "Oh my goodness! Look at that! Time is passing! Before you know it, there will only be two thousand one hundred and fifty-nine days left. Our first day is passing by and we haven't even learned a thing yet! What do you say we get this learning train started."

She reaches into her desk drawer and pulls out the old, navy blue train conductor's cap. For the thirty-first and last time she puts it on. She pumps her hand twice. "Toot! Toot! All aboard the Learning Train! First stop, Writing My Own Name! Who's coming aboard?"

Twenty-six hands shoot into the air. And Zinkoff, jumping to his feet so fast that he knocks his desk over with a nerve-slapping racket, thrusts up his hands and bellows to the ceiling: "YAHOO!"

Jerry Spinelli, *Loser* (New York: HarperCollins Children's Books, 2002), pp. 16–17.

BARELY ANY VOICE. **1 2 3 4 5 6** STRONG, CLEAR VOICE!

Words that describe this voice: _____

_____

The Defining Moment

Now is the moment to write your own definition of *voice.*
Your definition will help you evaluate your writing and
adjust your voice to fit the topic.

My Definition of Voice

_____

_____

_____

_____

Share and Compare

It's time to share your definition with one or more classmates.
Did you note any similarities to your definition? Differences?

One similarity I heard: _____

_____

One idea I hadn't thought of: _____

_____

A Writer's Question

**Which three to five words are the key
words in your definition? Write them here
and then read them aloud. The next time
you write, use these key words to focus
your attention on voice.**

_____

_____

_____

name: .... date: ....

Keeping Readers Connected

As a writer, you want your audience to feel connected to your ideas. This is especially important in *informational* writing, the reports and essays that you do for science, history, math, and English classes. Informational writing is based on what you have learned through research, experience, or analysis. What voice does this type of writing need? The voice of confidence—confidence that comes from writers who know their topics well.

Sharing an Example: The Endurance: Shackleton's Legendary Antarctic Expedition

On page 47 is a passage from Caroline Alexander's book, *The* Endurance: *Shackleton's Legendary Antarctic Expedition.* This book is a true account of the 1914 attempt by Ernest Shackleton and his crew to cross the Antarctic continent on foot. They managed to sail to within eighty-five miles of their destination before their ship, *Endurance,* became trapped in pack ice. This passage describes the ship's last moments, just before the ship is finally crushed by the powerful ice.

The *Endurance* had quieted, but that evening an unsettling incident occurred while several sailors were on deck. A band of eight emperor penguins solemnly approached, an unusually large number to be traveling together. Intently regarding the ship for some moments, they threw back their heads and emitted an eerie, soulful cry.

"I myself must confess that I have never, either before or since, heard them make any sound similar to the sinister wailings they moaned that day," wrote Worsley. "I cannot explain the incident." It was as if the emperors had sung the ship's dirge. McLeod, the most superstitious of the seamen, turned to Macklin and said, "Do you hear that? We'll none of us get back to our homes again."

Caroline Alexander, *The* Endurance: *Shackleton's Legendary Antarctic Expedition* (New York: Alfred A. Knopf, 1998), pp. 88–89.

Thoughts and Reactions

If you feel the passage by Caroline Alexander *does* have strong voice, write at least two things that the author did to give her writing strong voice. If you feel that the voice is too watered down, write at least two things the author *could have done* to strengthen her voice.

1. _____

2. _____

Reading, Rating, and Ranking

Read the following samples of informational writing to get a feeling for the voice. Then refer to the chart to rate each voice. When you've read and rated all three, rank them (strongest to weakest) based on the voice. (Ranking Tip: Rank the *voice,* not the topic.)

voice? 1 2 3 4 5 6 VOICE!

Flat and lifeless.   Energetic and informative.

Sample A

The Biggest, Fattest, and Longest Snakes _____

Some snakes are really thin, and some snakes are really big around. The biggest snakes come from the boa and python families, which include anacondas. Green anacondas are really heavy, up to 400 pounds. These snakes move faster in water. Pythons, at 29 feet, are the longest snakes and can eat large animals, such as deer. It's hard to measure snakes because they usually coil their bodies when they are picked up, but they stretch quite easily when they are dead.

Sample B

Conquering a Downed Power Line _____

You're driving down the road with your family in the middle of a terrible storm. The wind is howling, blowing the tall trees that line the road back and forth in a wild dance. A pounding rain hammers the car faster than the slapping windshield wipers can handle. Suddenly, a traffic light crashes to the ground, and the snakelike power line slams across the hood of your car. Instinctively, you reach for the door handle, but should you step out? Remember: Whether or not that power line touching your car is sparking, you should assume that it is alive with deadly electric current. Electricity can travel instantly through any conductive substance, such as the rainwater outside your car. That first step out the door could very well be your last. Keep everyone calm, stay in the car, and wait for help. These actions could save your life.

Sample C

Games and Violence _____

Video games and computer games aren't as bad as some people think they are. Some people think that kids who play violent games will go out into the world and do bad things. That could happen, but it probably won't. Scientists and people who study things like this can show that good things can happen to kids or adults who play these games. Better reflexes, better hand-to-eye coordination, and having fun are all good things. When people play these games, they aren't out on the streets doing bad things or aren't out in the sunlight where they could get burned. Video and computer games are really helpful in society.

Ranking the Voices

Briefly review the ratings you gave each of the three voices before ranking them. Remember to rank the voice behind the information.

Strongest Voice: Sample _____

Middle of the Pack Voice: Sample _____

Distant, Encyclopedic Voice: Sample _____

Revising to Strengthen Voice

Choose one of the two samples that you ranked as weak in voice. Think about what you could do to help readers connect. Mark any changes you want directly on the passage; then complete your revision on a separate sheet of paper.

A Writer's Question

What do you think is the key to creating and maintaining voice in informational writing?

name: .... date: ....

Thinking About Audience

Imagine that you're headed to a concert headlined by your favorite musical group. The curtain rises, the spotlight hits the band, and, to your amazement, the musicians begin playing a polka instead of your favorite songs. Are you disappointed, confused, or even annoyed? You bet! Instead of the special music you thought you'd be hearing, you got the wrong sound, the wrong beat—the wrong *voice.* Like entertainers, writers need to satisfy the audience if they want to be successful.

Sharing an Example: Animal Farm

Here's a short passage from George Orwell's classic book, *Animal Farm.* This book, as you may know, is about a group of overworked, underfed, and otherwise mistreated animals who rebel and take over the farm from their cruel master, Jones. The animals want to create a world based on justice and equality. Soon, though, the pigs who have taken charge of the farm are behaving a lot like Jones. Squealer, the pig's spokesperson, has to find just the right voice to explain to the other animals why the pigs are getting better food. Does he use his voice to get the response he wants?

"Comrades!" he cried. "You do not imagine, I hope, that we pigs are doing this in a spirit of selfishness and privilege? Many of us actually dislike milk and apples. I dislike them myself. Our sole object in taking these things is to preserve our health. Milk and apples (this has been proven by Science, comrades) contain substances absolutely necessary to the well-being of a pig. We pigs are brainworkers. The whole management and organisation of this farm depend on us. Day and night we are watching over your welfare. It is for *your* sake that we drink that milk and eat those apples. Do you know what would happen if we pigs failed in our duty? Jones would come back! Yes, Jones would come back! Surely, comrades," cried Squealer almost pleadingly, skipping from side to side and whisking his tail, "surely there is no one among you who wants to see Jones come back?"

Now if there was one thing that the animals were completely certain of, it was that they did not want Jones back. When it was put to them in this light, they had no more to say.

George Orwell, *Animal Farm* (New York: Signet Classics, 1956), pp. 52–53.

Reflecting

Squealer was able to get what he wanted from his audience: cooperation. How did he use voice to accomplish this? Write your ideas here:

_____

_____

How would you describe Squealer's voice in this situation? Write two or three descriptive words.

_____

_____

_____

Changing the Audience, Changing the Voice

Squealer used a certain voice to speak to the other farm animals. If his audience had been his fellow ruling pigs, what sort of voice might he have used? Become Squealer for three or four sentences, using a voice different from the one you heard in *Animal Farm*. Write what Squealer might say to the other pigs.

_____

_____

_____

_____

_____

_____

_____

_____

_____

Share and Compare

Share your new Squealer voice with a partner; then compare the voices. Are there any similarities? How would you describe your version of Squealer's voice?

I would describe Squealer's new voice as _____

or _____ .

Flexing Your Voice

Now that you're focused on voice and audience, you will write two letters, one to a parent or guardian and the other to a relative or a friend. In each letter, you'll ask for money for a new skateboard, some special clothing, or some other nonessential item. Each letter must be at least eight sentences long. Think about the differences, subtle as they may be, in your two audiences. Don't forget that the details you include and the words you use affect the voices you create.

_____

_____

_____

_____

_____

_____

_____

_____

_____

_____

_____

_____

_____

_____

_____

Share and Compare

Meet with a partner, and share your two letters. To make sure that you're concentrating on the appropriate voice for each audience, don't share the greetings as you read your letters aloud. See whether your partner can identify the audience for each letter.

A Writer's Question

We all use different speaking voices with different audiences—grandparents, brothers or sisters, teachers, police officers, friends. How do the ways you shift your speaking voice match the ways you shift your written voice?

Kick It into High Gear!

Writing fueled by a powerful voice takes readers on a fantastic ride through a range of emotions. In contrast, writing that sputters along, barely running on the fumes of a weak voice, will disappoint readers hoping for a more adventurous ride. But here's the good news: flat, voiceless writing can be refueled through revision.

Sharing an Example: Meely LaBauve

As the primary energy source for strong writing, voice is an amazing fuel that can spark anger, happiness, humor, tension, confidence, and other feelings. Read this short passage from *Meely LaBauve* by Ken Wells. It's the story of fifteen-year-old Emile LaBauve, known as Meely, who is growing up in Catahoula Bayou, Louisiana. As you read, ask yourself, "How much voice does this passage have?" and "Where does the voice come from?"

Sample 1

There's a great blue heron that stays over on the far bank near that cypress, huntin' minnows in the shallows. I see him pretty much every time I'm here. He used to fly away but he don't no more.

Curious bird he is, walkin' slow as winter on them stilt legs till he sees somethin', then peckin' like lightnin'. I'm glad I'm not a minnow.

The other reason I like fishin' the Perch Hole is that there ain't no *choupique* in here. Don't git me wrong—*choupique* is the best fightin' fish there is in these waters. But I won't eat 'em normally 'cause they're seriously ugly and they taste like the swamp, though if I'm hungry enough I'll eat whatever there is.

As Daddy says, a hungry man ain't normally a picky man.

A lot of the ole Cajuns like *choupique,* though. They'll grind 'em up into meatballs. Some people figger that with enough cayenne, bay leaf, and shallots, you could eat ground-up mule. And I guess you could.

Daddy don't like to eat *choupique,* either, 'less he's desperate, but for a different reason. He says *choupique* are like dinosaurs. They've been around about as long as the bayou itself, and somethin' so old shouldn't be messed with.

Daddy has peculiar notions.

Ken Wells, *Meely LaBauve* (New York: Random House, 2000), pp. 29–30.

Messin' with the Voice

What if, in Meely's words, we messed with the voice and rewrote this excerpt, draining out most of the fuel (energy)? With apologies to Mr. Wells, it might sound like this:

Sample 2

I like fishing the Perch Hole because there are a lot of animals there, such as birds. The Perch Hole doesn't have any *choupique.* They are great fighting fish, but they are ugly and don't taste good. Some people will eat *choupique* if they can put in enough seasoning. My father is not very fond of *choupique* either. He says they shouldn't be bothered because they've been around so long. He has interesting ideas.

Seeing and Hearing the Difference

To remove the voice, we eliminated many descriptive words and phrases, as well as the conversational style and dialect. Did these changes affect what you saw and heard? Carefully compare the two samples, asking yourself what you see and feel as you read each sample.

Sample 1—*Meely LaBauve*—Fuel Tank Full

I can see _____.

I can hear _____.

Sample 2—*Meely LaBauve "revision"*—Running on Fumes

I can see _____.

I can hear _____.

Where's the "Fuel" Coming From?

It's likely that Sample 1 created sharper sensations for you as a reader. Sample 1 does have more voice, but what, specifically, did author Ken Wells do to create energy in this passage? Write at least three specific strategies the author used to give his original passage strong voice.

1. _____

2. _____

3. _____

Shifting into High Gear

This next piece of writing needs help. Energize this voiceless sample. Read the piece carefully with a pen or pencil in hand. Mark any sections or phrases that you feel need help. Revise them as necessary to give this piece strong voice.

Repair Manual Tip:
Review the strategies used by Ken Wells in *Meely LaBauve.* Put some of the same strategies to work as you revise. You could also recall your personal definition of voice.

Pro Football Camp

Last July, during my trip to my grandparents' house in Chattaroy, Washington, Gram and Gramps took me to watch the Seattle Seahawks practice in a nearby city. I had never seen a professional football team practice. It was really cool. The weather was pretty hot, so the coaches let the players take a lot of water breaks. There were a lot of veteran players I recognized and a bunch of rookies, too.

There were a lot of people watching the players practice. At different times, people would shout encouragement to a player they knew or liked. Sometimes they would tease a rookie for making a mistake.

At the end of the practice, the players walked right by us. A lot of them stopped along the fence to sign autographs. Some of those guys were huge! I had brought a hat with me for players to sign. The coach even signed some autographs.

Write your revised version here.

_____

_____

_____

_____

_____

_____

_____

_____

_____

A Writer's Question

Is voice a matter of attitude toward your topic, or is it more about strategies? Is it both? Explain your answer.

Unit 4
Word Choice

Imagine that you're making your way through the cafeteria line when a friend suddenly grabs your plate and says, "Here—let me get some food for you!" Before you know it, you're looking at a huge slice of liver, a few pickles, several dozen Brussels sprouts, and a side of oatmeal. You politely tell your friend, "Gee, I was thinking of a slice of pizza, with maybe a salad and soda." She looks very puzzled, as if you've lost your wits. "Come *on,*" is her response. "Food is food, isn't it?" Well, not exactly. As you'll discover in this unit, good writers are every bit as careful about their word selection as even the fussiest eater is about food. They don't overload their "plates," and they don't settle for whatever is handy. Words, like foods, have their own textures and flavors.

In this unit, you'll have a chance to nurture your writing. You will learn to choose words that convey precisely what you want to say by

◆ using synonyms and antonyms with flair

◆ harnessing the power of sensory words

◆ choosing precise words

◆ cutting the clutter

Choosing the Right Words

Good writers know that with a little patience and the help of a dictionary and a thesaurus, they can find the right words to create lively and imaginative "pictures" for readers. So make sure your dictionary and thesaurus are nearby, and get ready to stretch your vocabulary and your writing ability.

Sharing an Example: The Hostile Hospital

The Hostile Hospital, the eighth book in the "Unfortunate Events" series, continues the struggles of Violet, Klaus, and Sunny Beaudelaire to keep their family fortune from the clutches of their distant relative, the evil Count Olaf. As you read this passage, see whether you can get a feel for the author's love of words and his playful way of speaking directly to the reader. Pay particular attention to the word *spurious.*

"Let's go," Klaus said, and put his hand on the door of the supply closet. But he did not open it. Instead he turned back to his sister, and the two Beaudelaires looked at each other. Even though the siblings were wearing white coats, and had surgical masks on their faces, they did not look like doctors. They looked like two children in white coats with surgical masks on their faces. Their disguises looked spurious —a word which here means "nothing at all like a real doctor"—and yet they were no more spurious than the disguises that Olaf had been using since his first attempt to steal the Beaudelaire fortune. Klaus and Sunny looked at one another and hoped that Olaf's methods would work for them, and help them steal their sister, and without another word, they opened the door and stepped out of the supply closet.

Lemony Snicket, *The Hostile Hospital* (New York: HarperCollins, 2001), p. 164.

Reflect

From the author's use of the word *spurious* and his situational definition, what do you think the word means?

I think *spurious* means _____

_____ .

Next, go to your thesaurus and look up *spurious*. Write down three or four synonyms. Put a star by the word that best fits the author's idea and voice.

Synonyms for *spurious* (adjective)

1. _____   3. _____

2. _____   4. _____

The Right Color

Artists choose certain colors to paint the picture they want viewers to see. Writers do the same thing with words. Just as green can be forest green, moss green, or lime green, each word has a slightly different shade of meaning. Read the following three sentences.

He was **angry** about the broken window.

He was **furious** about the broken window.

He was **annoyed** about the broken window.

Angry, furious, and *annoyed* are synonyms, but does each reveal the same level of feeling about the broken window? Imagine these words as "degrees," and place them on the "word thermometer." Put the "coolest" word on the bottom and the "hottest" word on the top.

To extend your understanding of shades of meaning, use your thesaurus to find **antonyms** for *angry, furious,* and *annoyed.* Make sure your choices match the level of intensity of the three words given, and place them on the word thermometer.

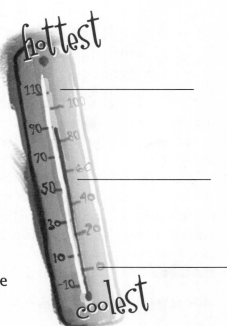

Extending Your Practice: More Choices

Here's another passage from *The Hostile Hospital.* Using a thesaurus, first identify the part of speech of each word in color. Then list two or three synonyms for each word. Note that you can replace a single word with a phrase. The reverse is also true.

Because most doctors are adults, the white coats were far too big for the children, who were reminded of the enormous pinstripe suits Esmè Squalor had purchased for them when she had been their guardian. Klaus helped Sunny roll up the sleeves of her coat, and Sunny helped Klaus tie his mask around his face, and in a few moments the children were finished putting on their disguises.

Word	Part of Speech	Synonyms
1. _____		_____ , _____ , _____
2. _____		_____ , _____ , _____
3. _____		_____ , _____ , _____
4. _____		_____ , _____ , _____

Matching Shades

Look over your synonyms and circle the word on each list that you think is the closest match in meaning and intensity to the word the author selected. Then complete the passage below using the words you circled.

Because most doctors are adults, the white coats were far too big for the children, who were reminded of the _____ *(enormous)* pinstripe suits Esmè Squalor had _____ *(purchased)* for them when she had been their _____ *(guardian)*. Klaus helped Sunny roll up the sleeves of her coat, and Sunny helped Klaus tie his mask around his face, and in a few moments the children were finished _____ *(putting on)* their disguises.

Playing with Opposites

Let's try another passage. This time, with your thesaurus, replace the author's words with antonyms that are *farthest* away in meaning and intensity from the originals. (**HINT:** Remember to retain the part of speech—noun, verb, adjective, and so on.)

The night sky seemed _____ *(alive)*. _____ *(Fierce)* winds

_____ *(howled)* _____ *(violently)* around the windows and roof,

_____ *(threatening)* us as we _____ *(huddled)* inside,

_____ *(terrified)*. At last, like a _____ *(disgruntled)*

_____ *(tyrant)*, the storm _____ *(raged)* over the

_____ *(mountains)*.

A Writer's Question

In this lesson you have been using a dictionary and a thesaurus to expand the "word bank" in your brain. What other ways can a writer stretch his or her vocabulary?

name: .... date: ....

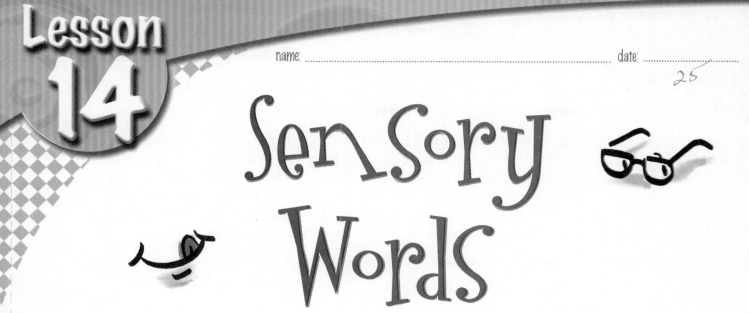

Sensory Words

Sensory language—words and phrases that trigger the senses of touch, sight, taste, smell, and hearing—can bring readers into the writer's world. Readers attach to sensory language the way mountain climbers cling to a foothold. Through sensory language, readers see what you see, hear what you hear, feel what you feel. Let's explore some strategies for making the climb easy.

Sharing an Example: The Fellowship of the Ring

Here's an example of sensory language used in a passage from J.R.R. Tolkien's classic fantasy tale, *The Fellowship of the Ring.* Read the passage, looking and listening carefully for the sensory words that invite you into the author's world. Underline any sensory words you find.

At the south end of the greensward there was an opening. There the green floor ran on into the wood, and formed a wide space like a hall, roofed by the boughs of trees. Their great trunks ran like pillars down each side. In the middle there was a wood-fire blazing, and upon the tree-pillars torches with lights of gold and silver were burning steadily. The elves sat round the fire upon the grass or upon the sawn rings of old trunks. Some went to and fro bearing cups and pouring drink; others brought food on heaped plates and dishes.

"This is poor fare," they said to the hobbits; "for we are lodging in the greenwood far from our halls. If ever you are our guests at home, we will treat you better."

95

"It seems to me good enough for a birthday-party," said Frodo.

Pippin afterwards recalled little of either food or drink, for his mind was filled with the light upon the elf-faces, and the sound of voices so various and so beautiful that he felt in a waking dream. But he remembered that there was bread, surpassing the savour of a fair white loaf to one who is starving; and fruits sweet as wildberries and richer than the tended fruits of gardens; he drained a cup that was filled with a fragrant draught, cool as a clear fountain, golden as a summer afternoon.

J.R.R. Tolkien, *The Fellowship of the Ring* (New York: Houghton Mifflin, 1954), pp. 80–81.

Sensory Reaction

Look again at the sensory words you underlined before comparing your findings with the chart below. Add any words that are missing from the chart.

I see	I hear	I feel	I smell	I taste
great trunks	elf-speech	wood-fire blazing	wood-fire blazing	bread
wood-fire blazing	talking with delight	tree-pillars	bread	fruits sweet as wildberries

Working from Scratch

Here's a passage from *A Step from Heaven,* by An Na. The story centers on Young Ju and her family's emigration from Korea to the United States. In this part, Young Ju and her little brother Joon are waiting in the car for their parents, both of whom are working late at their second jobs. Read the passage carefully, underlining any words or phrases that are good examples of sensory language. Then list each detail on the chart that follows the passage.

And right before the sun goes down, before the rush of knives chopping, food flying, and "Order ready!" singing out, Uhmma will come out of the kitchen and give us our dinner. If we are lucky, it might be ginger chicken, spicy hot, fire on the tongue. But most times it is soup and rice in a bowl, all mixed together so you

95

can eat it with one big spoon. Joon and I sit on the curb with our bowls balanced on our knees, slurping like we are not supposed to at the dinner table. We laugh and see who can make the grossest noise.

But today, because it is raining and the cars are pulling off the freeway quick quick for a long, early dinner, Uhmma can only rush out with two dry old hamburgers and a big carton of milk. After we finish our dinner, Joon can't sit still. He crawls around in the back seat sticking his hand down between the seat cushions for change. After he finds only two dimes, Joon bounces the soccer ball off the ceiling and starts to sing. Soon the whole car is rocking with his crazy song. "Spider-Man, Spider-Man. He can do what no one can."

An Na, *A Step from Heaven* (Asheville: Front Street, 2001), pp. 62–63.

I see	I hear	I feel	I smell	I taste

Your Turn to Extend the Invitation

Imagine yourself, as An Na did, waiting for your parents alone or with a brother or sister. Where are you? What are you doing, thinking, feeling, hearing, smelling, noticing in the world around you as you wait—and wait? Begin with a little prewriting, making some notes about the sensory details that will give readers a foothold on your world.

I see	I hear	I feel	I smell	I taste

Now, select the strongest of your sensory notes and put them together in a descriptive paragraph (at least eight sentences) or a poem. Invite readers inside your world by sharing what you see, hear, taste, smell, or feel.

_____

_____

_____

_____

_____

_____

_____

_____

_____

_____

_____

_____

_____

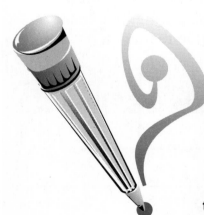

A Writer's Question

Picture yourself visiting an Internet site devoted to tropical vacations. Unfortunately, the Web site has no photographs and uses no sensory language to describe the vacation destinations. You find only the names of some islands. Would you spend your money on an island vacation and hope for the best? Forget the whole thing? Switch to another site? Explain your answer.

Lesson 15

name: .... date: ....

Call It as You See It

If you were umpiring a baseball game, you would need to pay close attention to the action, keep your eye on the ball at all times, and do your best to "call it as you see it." Writers have the same obligation. They need to "call it as they see it," too. Let's say you're thinking, "cherry red, ground-hugging Italian sports car," but you write "car." Now your readers have to fill in their own details. That's like an umpire calling out, "Pitch one!" without specifying a ball or a strike. Use the precise words you need. Call it as you see it.

"pitch one."

Sharing an Example: Zack and The Hungry Ocean

Here are two short writing examples, one from a novel and the other from a nonfiction book. As you read each passage, underline any words or phrases that you think are particularly precise, vivid, or energetic.

Example 1

I was used to going to school through the rumble and snarl of traffic, sidewalks teeming with people. . . . I had traveled on a city bus jammed with faces of every color and humming with languages from around the world. Now each morning I stood like a stump at the end of our unpaved driveway waiting for the big yellow monster to swallow me up and transport me to Boredom High School. I had been dragged from a major street in the biggest city in the country to the edge of the known universe, a rural route in Garafraxa Township—the name sounded like an incurable skin disease—with a chicken farm at the dead end, on the outskirts of a no-place village called Fergus where, as near as I could tell, the locals' idea of a good time was trying on gloves at the department store or watching the blue light revolve on the top of the snowplow.

There was nothing funny about being the only child of two stubborn parents who had decided to leave the city and do the pioneer thing among the trees.

William Bell, *Zack* (New York: Simon & Schuster Books for Young Readers, 1999), pp. 7–8.

Example 2

I woke up one morning, at the age of twelve, to the smell of low tide. The scent of seaweed and tidal pools crept through my open bedroom window and tiptoed around the room, not overpowering, but arousing interest. Usually awakening to the faint smell of pine and the rush of wind in the trees, that day I was intrigued with the thick, musty odor of sun-baked salt and mussel-covered rocks. My ears strained to pick up the slight sloshing of the tide as it swept in and out around the low-water-mark rocks and ledges. It seemed strange that having been surrounded by the ocean my entire life, this was the first time I noticed the screeching of the gulls and the drone of a diesel-powered lobster boat nearby.

Linda Greenlaw, *The Hungry Ocean* (New York: Hyperion, 1999), p. 52.

Share and Compare

Meet with a partner to share and compare your underlined words and phrases. Did you find some of the same vivid, specific language? Write at least four words or phrases that you underlined.

Zack: Vivid, Specific Language

1. *rumble and snarl of traffic* _____

2. _____

3. _____

4. _____

The Hungry Ocean: Vivid, Specific Language

1. *scent of seaweed and tidal pools* _____

2. _____

3. _____

4. _____

Flat to Vivid

Any writer can create flat, dull language, but it takes effort to write something memorable and specific. Here are two flat sentences in need of revision. As you read each sentence, circle any general, lifeless language. Then, revise each sentence by finding energetic, specific, interesting language to take its place. One example has been done for you.

Example Sentence—

Flat: The (boy had fun) in the (sand.)

Vivid: When the tide had gone out, Andrew spent hours building a city with the bleached shells and sticks he collected along the shore.

1. **Flat:** I like the food at this one restaurant in my town.

   Vivid: _____

   _____.

2. **Flat:** We go to this place nearby to do things when the

   weather is bad.

   Vivid: _____

   _____.

Share and Compare

With your partner, share and compare your revised sentences. Did both of you create clearer, more inviting pictures with your revisions? Rate yourselves here.

_____ Very inviting and vivid—our added details create sharp, clear pictures.

_____ Some improvement—the picture is coming into focus.

_____ Not much better—our changes are still too general.

Energetic Writing of Your Own

Now you're ready to create some precise, vivid writing of
your own. For this practice, you may either (1) describe a
place that holds strong memories for you, such as a house
or neighborhood you used to live in, a summer camping spot,
or the ocean or (2) tell about a time you were upset with a
decision that someone made. It might be helpful to do some
prewriting—detail list, picture, word web, see/feel T-table—to
find the vivid language you need. Your writing should consist
of at least eight sentences.

_____

_____

_____

_____

_____

_____

_____

_____

Share and Compare

Before you meet with your partner, read through your sentences
once more. Look and listen carefully for any vague, flat words or
phrases, and replace them with specific and energetic language.

A Writer's Question

**What would you say to someone who
thinks it's just too much trouble to make
writing specific and energetic? Write a
brief note here.**

_____

_____

_____

Lesson 16

name: .... date: ....

The Right Team for the Job

Imagine all the words in your writer's vocabulary lined up like soldiers waiting for the signal to parachute onto a training field. It's time to write; your word soldiers are more than ready, and they all want to go. What happens to your writing, though, if you release them all at once? All the words you know descend on the blank page, cluttering your writing and overwhelming your readers. The mission—creating clear meaning and vivid images—is a total failure. You needed a carefully selected team, not a whole battalion. Not every word is right for every mission. You need to pick just the right team.

Sharing an Example

Every time you write, your mission is to communicate with your readers. Bury the message under clutter, and readers may never uncover your main idea. Read the following sample and ask yourself, "Is this message clear, or did this writer send in too many word soldiers for the task?"

Summer football conditioning camp began yesterday, Monday, August 5, and will last through Friday, August 9, the first full week of August. Football conditioning camp is sponsored, organized, and run by the local youth football association and the varsity head football coach of our local neighborhood high school. Camp goes from late afternoon until early evening before it gets dark, 5:30 P.M. to 8:00 P.M. in the evening. The camp is for anybody, really, but you have to be going into grade three, four, five, six, seven, or eight. You don't have to have any previous football experience to go to camp, but it probably helps if you have had some previous football experience with throwing, catching, blocking, and tackling. If you haven't had much experience, the camp's purpose is to teach about the basics of football—throwing, catching, blocking, tackling, and running. One fun thing about football conditioning camp is that it is one chance, or opportunity, to hang out with lots of people you know, like your friends and other people you may know from school or the neighborhood. I finished seventh grade last year, so now I'm going into grade eight. This is now my fourth time at summer conditioning camp for me. I started when I was going into the fifth grade, which was my first year of camp. Before that, I played another sport, soccer, not football, but I quit soccer in the fifth grade to be able to try football. From the time school gets out until the first full week in August, I don't think about anything except football and going to my favorite thing, football conditioning camp.

Reaction

How would you rate this piece of writing?

_____ It's about right—actually, the writer might want to say a little *more* about football conditioning camp.

_____ It's a bit wordy, but the writer wants readers to understand the message.

_____ Clutter with a capital *C!*

Now read the passage aloud. Listen and watch for clutter. As you read, cross out any unnecessary words, phrases, or sentences; then revise, using carefully selected words or making slight changes in wording. When you have finished, read the passage aloud once more to be sure you've used just the right words—and no more.

A Little Comparison

Compare the revision below with your paragraph. Do they look
and sound similar? Did you find more changes to make? Did
you use fewer words?

Summer football conditioning camp began yesterday, August 5, and will end
on Friday, August 9. Camp lasts from 5:30 to 8:00 P.M. and is run by the local
youth football association and the varsity football coach from our neighborhood
high school. The camp is for anybody in grades three through eight, regardless
of football experience. The camp's purpose is to teach the basics of football:
throwing, catching, blocking, tackling, and running. This is my fourth time at
camp; I started when I was going into the fifth grade. From the time school gets
out, I don't think about anything except football conditioning camp.

Share and Compare

Quickly compare revisions. Examine both paragraphs, and then
put a check next to the sentence that best describes the
comparisons.

_____ We slashed even *more*—ours is down to a few sentences.

_____ We cut out *almost* the same amount.

_____ We found *less to cut,* but we still like our revision.

_____ We found *less to cut* and decided we would cut more
next time.

Eliminating Clutter

Read this next sample, and eliminate any clutter. When you've
finished cutting, rewrite the paragraph in its more precise
form. You may change the structure or punctuation of
sentences to make your final revision read smoothly.

About a week ago, in the middle of last week, my brother, younger brother to be
exact, rediscovered his bicycle as if it had been lost for a long time, and he finally
found it. I'm not sure exactly what the reason is for his recent compulsion to ride
up and down the street in front of our house in our neighborhood. Whatever is
behind it, he's a maniac, and now because of my little brother, the crazy person, I

have to ride my bike pretty much whenever he rides his. He rides his bike almost constantly, and my parents, Mom and Dad, think that he needs a guardian to watch over him and supervise his rides. As you can imagine, I have other things to do, being older and wiser, besides being a bike monitor for Mr. Tour de Neighborhood over and over again. I've had to put my life on hold—no phone, friends, games, reading, because I actually like to read—to serve as biking boy's private highway patrol. Perhaps, just maybe, I think I might have to sabotage his bike if I'm ever going to get my life back.

_____

_____

_____

_____

_____

_____

_____

_____

Share and Compare

Share your revision with a partner. What changes did each of you make? Did you see or hear any clutter that did not have to be cut? Discuss how you went about deciding what to eliminate.

A Writer's Question

What is the best way to find clutter?

Sentence Fluency

If you have ever danced with someone, you know how important it is to be aware of your partner as you move together. Imagine yourself out on the dance floor, having a great time, when suddenly your partner stomps on your feet or changes rhythm without warning. You'd probably find yourself looking for a new partner. In the same way, a reader will soon abandon any writer who starts and stops sporadically or otherwise interrupts a smooth, fluent flow of text. Like accomplished dancers, good writers create a rhythm and flow that is easy to follow.

In this unit, you'll practice some strategies for creating text that readers will be able to follow. You will learn about

◆ varying sentence beginnings

◆ using transitional words and phrases with restraint

◆ identifying flowing, fluent writing

◆ writing fluently

My Shoes... My Shoes... My Shoes...

"My shoes are the latest thing. My shoes will help me run faster. My shoes are worn only by the best players. My shoes took all of my summer savings to buy. . . ."**

Want to hear more? These shoes may thrill the writer, but most readers are unlikely to care about them. Repetition is both unnecessary and boring, and good writers will avoid it. They know that varying sentence beginnings not only adds interest but also helps readers focus on the message.

Sharing an Example: After Hamelin

In *After Hamelin,* author Bill Richardson uses the legend of the Pied Piper as a springboard for a new, imaginative tale. The book tells the story of Penelope, who awakens on her eleventh birthday to discover that she has lost her hearing. The Pied Piper rid her city of rats but was never paid the gold he was promised. He uses his hypnotic music to lure the children of Hamelin away, but Penelope is left behind because she cannot hear the song. Read the passage silently, paying close attention to the highlighted sentence beginnings.

I am a harper's daughter. In our house, for as long as I could remember, the thrum and ring of the harp had been as common a sound as the clatter of dishes or the slamming of a door. Everyone knew there was no harper finer than my father. Banquets, festivals, state occasions: none would be complete if the virtuoso Govan were not on hand to strike the harp.

His fame was widespread. Apprentices came from near and far to study with him. There was always a young man staying in our attic room. Sometimes, if they were homesick, they would talk in their sleep. I would wake in the night and hear them moaning sad-sounding words in Italian, Spanish, Welsh, Portuguese. Not even the Plague kept them away. They were willing to put up with rats gnawing their shoes and chewing their strings so they might learn to play, and also learn how to make the harps for which my father was so celebrated.

From far and near they came, with all their talent and all their yearning. But no one, no matter how gifted, was able to convince a harp to sing as true as Govan. And no one, no matter how diligently he worked, was able to make a harp with a voice as pure as one crafted by the master. The Maestro. That is what they called Govan. The Maestro. He could charm the music out of wood. No one, Govan least of all, could explain how he awakened the melody in balsam or beech or fir.

Bill Richardson, *After Hamelin* (Toronto: Annick Press, Ltd., 2000), pp. 13–14.

Your Response

How much variety did you notice in the beginnings of Bill Richardson's sentences?

_____ A great deal of variety

_____ Some variety

_____ Almost no variety

Read the passage aloud. What do you notice about the sound and flow of the author's sentences? Imagine that Richardson had written, "Govan is my father. Govan is the finest harper around. Govan's fame was widespread. Govan attracted apprentices from near and far." Would the passage be as interesting or have the same fluency? What would happen to your involvement as a reader?

_____

_____

Revising "The Softball Championship Series"

Here's a sample of writing with a fluency problem. Before you read it, underline or highlight the first three or four words of each sentence. Then, read the passage aloud to get a better idea of the sound and flow of the writing.

The Softball Championship Series

My softball team advanced to the championship series for the first time in school history. My softball team had to travel to Sacramento, California, for the big tournament. My team was so excited to get to play for the title, even after we found out which teams were in our bracket. My softball team had to win its first two games against the teams who had won the tournament nine of the last ten years. We decided to use this as our motivation rather than let it get us down. My team's first game was against the current champion, a team from Texas. My softball team really came through when it counted. My team hit and pitched the best it had all year and won the game, one to zero. My softball team used this big win to propel us through our other games. My softball team won the rest of its games to earn the chance to play for the title. My softball team fought hard in the championship, but we lost a tough game, six to one.

Beginning with Variety

How did you like reading this passage? Did the lack of fluency affect your interest in and enthusiasm for the topic? Revise the softball passage to create more interest and better fluency by varying the sentence beginnings. You may replace or add words or rearrange words within each sentence. Remember that changes you make may require changes in punctuation. Also, think "purposeful variety"; not every sentence needs to begin differently. Sentence beginnings should help the reader follow the flow.

_____

_____

_____

_____

_____

_____

_____

_____

_____

_____

_____

Share and Compare

The best way to appreciate the fluency in writing is to hear the words read aloud. Meet with a partner and take turns reading your revised paragraphs aloud, comparing them to the original. With your partner's help, rate your revised paragraph:

_____ A real improvement! I used a variety of beginnings to create a more fluent paragraph.

_____ Some improvement. I made a few changes, but more are needed.

_____ Not much improvement. The sentences sound about the same as they did. The sentences still begin the same way.

A Writer's Question

Is repetition ever a good idea? In some cases, could repetition actually enhance fluency? When? How? (Can you think of an example in either prose or poetry?)

name: .... date: ....

Trucking in the Transitions

Too much time in the bright sun can cause sunburn.
Too many spicy peppers in your favorite food can cause
an upset stomach. Everything has its limits, even good
transitions. It's helpful to link ideas together in thoughtful
ways, but if you really want to avoid upsetting your
audience, don't overdo transitions such as *in other words,
as you can see, additionally, because,* and *therefore.*

Sharing an Example: All Quiet on the Western Front

Here is a passage from the classic World War I tale, *All Quiet on
the Western Front,* by Erich Maria Remarque. The war-weary
Katczinsky is sharing his army experience with Paul, the story's
narrator. We have altered the writing a bit, by adding far too
many transitional words and phrases. We've put the extras in
color to make them easier to spot. Carefully read the passage
aloud, looking and listening for how these extra transitions
affect fluency.

In himself then man is, more or less, essentially a beast, only, for the most part,
he butters it over moreover like a slice of bread with a little decorum, that is. The
army, to emphasize, is based on that; one man must always, therefore, have power
over the other, naturally. The mischief is meanwhile merely that each one, to begin
with, has much too much power, in the end. A non-com. can torment a private, a
lieutenant a non-com., a captain a lieutenant, until he goes mad. And because they
know they can, all in all, they all soon acquire the habit more or less. To illustrate,
take a simple case: we are marching back from the parade-ground dog-tired, truly,

then comes the order to sing, for instance. We sing spiritlessly, as a result, for it is all we can do to trudge along with our rifles. At once the company is turned about, that is, and has to do another hour's drill as punishment, however. On the march back, to repeat, the order to sing is given again, and once more we start. Now what's the use, after all, of all that? It's simply that the company commander's head, obviously, has been turned by having so much power. And throughout nobody blames him. On the contrary, he is praised for being strict . . . He can only do that in the army, for example. To sum it up, it goes to the heads of them all, you see. And the more insignificant, clearly, a man has been in civil life the worse it takes him, apparently."

Your Reaction

How did this passage sound to you as you read it aloud? Did it have an easy and natural flow? Could you determine the author's main idea, or did you find yourself tripping over transitions?

_____ This passage was a breeze to read and understand. The extra transitions really helped.

_____ There were a few confusing spots, but some of those extra transitions helped.

_____ All those extra words made the whole passage confusing.

The Original

Here's the passage the way the author wrote it. The extra transitional words and phrases have been removed. Read this version aloud, and then rate it on the scale that follows.

In himself man is essentially a beast, only he butters it over like a slice of bread with a little decorum. The army is based on that; one man must always have power over the other. The mischief is merely that each one has much too much power. A non-com. can torment a private, a lieutenant a non-com., a captain a lieutenant, until he goes mad. And because they know they can, they all soon acquire the habit more or less. Take a simple case: we are marching back from the parade-ground dog-tired, then comes the order to sing. We sing spiritlessly, for it is all we can do to trudge along with our rifles. At once the company is turned about and has to do another hour's drill as punishment. On the march back the order to sing is given again, and once more we start. Now what's the use of all that? It's simply that the company commander's head has been turned by having so much power.

And nobody blames him. On the contrary, he is praised for being strict . . . He can only do that in the army. It goes to the heads of them all, you see. And the more insignificant a man has been in civil life the worse it takes him.

Erich Maria Remarque, *All Quiet on the Western Front* (New York: Fawcett Crest, 1975), pp. 44–45.

_____ Without those extra transitions, it is very hard to connect the ideas. I really couldn't follow it.

_____ It's a little more fluent without the extra transitions, but I would have preferred to keep a few.

_____ This is much easier to follow without the extra transitions.

Too Many Transitions

Read the following piece aloud carefully, with a pen or pencil in hand. Delete unneeded transitions to keep the writing fluent.
Hint: Some transitions may help the flow of ideas. Don't cut them all.

Incredibly enough, it's that time of year again when smoke fills the sky and, in addition, news about wildfires fills the front pages, and to sum up, dominates the local TV news. For this reason, it's no surprise to see groups of young men and women, moreover, at the airport heading out, not surprisingly, to join hotshot crews destined for the fires' front lines. As of yesterday, there were still seven fires burning, even though crews have been out fighting the fires for weeks. Additionally, helicopters equipped with huge buckets used to dump water on the worst spots have been seen flying back and forth across the sky. Among those leaving the airport, nevertheless, are fire crew members finally returning for some badly needed rest.

Smoothing Things Out

Rewrite the forest fire piece, combining or rewriting sentences and changing wording slightly to keep the sentences flowing.
Hint: Read aloud as you go to make sure that your revision is both logical and expressive.

_____

_____

_____

_____

_____

_____

_____

_____

_____

Share and Compare

When you've finished revising, meet with a partner to share your improved paragraph. To compare the fluency before and after revising, one of you should read the original aloud. Then, take turns reading your revisions. What changes did you make? Did you improve fluency?

_____ I made the right number of changes.

_____ I changed a lot, but we heard more unneeded transitions as we read aloud.

_____ I cut a lot, but I still need to work on smoothing out the flow.

A Writer's Question

It's sometimes said that good writers develop an "ear" for fluency. Can your writer's "ear" tell you when you have enough of the right transitions? How? What's the secret to good balance?

name: .... date: ....

Famous for Flow

The Mississippi River is not known for starting and stopping like water from a faucet. It's famous for its flow, from Lake Itaska all the way to the Gulf of Mexico. As it flows, it twists and turns, meanders back and forth, and at times rolls toward the ocean in long, straight stretches. The best way to experience a river so majestic is up close, where you can see, hear, and feel its flowing power. Good writing is best experienced that same way. Fluent writing almost begs to be read aloud so that the rhythm and pacing can carry you along the way a river carries a raft.

Sharing an Example: Troy

Here's a short passage from *Troy*, by Adele Geras. The book is based on the story of the Trojan War, something you may have read about before. Read the passage aloud, softly. Think about the elements that make a piece of writing fluent. Then, complete the Elements of Fluency list that has been started for you.

Alastor opened his eyes and wondered for a moment if this was the kingdom of Hades. He was lying flat on his back on a thin pallet on the ground. This place was nowhere he recognized, but it smelled of men, sweating and bleeding, and there were sounds of groaning coming from somewhere. He tried to turn his head, but pain like knives heated on a blacksmith's fire and plunged into his neck stopped him, and he was left staring into the darkness about his head. He closed his eyes. Had he really seen him again: the Black Warrior, the one who had come so close to him on the battlefield? He'd been there, yes, yes he had . . . in the corner of this very room, staring at me from under the iron helmet, his eyes as cold as death. I remember, Alastor thought, exactly where I saw the Warrior before. He said his name was Ares.

Adele Geras, *Troy* (San Diego: Harcourt, 2000) p. 68.

Elements of Fluency: How do writers create fluency?

1. <u>They vary sentence beginnings to create and maintain interest.</u>

2. <u>They use transitional words and phrases to connect ideas.</u>

3. _____

4. _____

5. _____

6. _____

Measuring the Flow: Read and Rank

A good first step toward improving your writing is to assess the work of other writers for fluency. Here are three pieces to read and assess. Read each at least twice, aloud if possible. Later you will rank them from MOST to LEAST fluent.

Sample A

I don't know if I could live someplace that wasn't within at the most a two-hour drive from the beach. I like being close to the beach so that I can walk and squish the sand between my toes with the sound of the surf washing away stressful thoughts, which helps me recharge my batteries, as my dad likes to say. There's a place I like to go that no one knows about. I won't tell you where it is. I want it to stay my secret.

Sample B

Watching my little brother learn to ride his bike has been the most amazing experience of the summer. Being the older sister means that I try to lead by good example. What this means, of course, is that we occasionally fight like cats and dogs. Yet underneath it all, I do love him—which made it even scarier the other night when he crashed his bike. Drew called me out of the house to come watch how fast he could go, and I watched. He was looking right at me when he hit a bump in the sidewalk. Before I could move or gasp, he flew over the handlebars and hit the pavement. I stopped breathing. Then I heard him call my name, and I ran.

Sample C

Is it true that summer is almost over? Of course it's true. It's true that summer is almost over because all you have to do is look at the store ads in the paper and when they start having back to school sales then you know that summer is near the end and that school is about to start. This doesn't make me very happy. This is not because I don't like school. This is because I like the freedom of summer. My bike. Camping with my friends. How do you feel about summer? If you feel like me then you'll understand how I feel.

Fluency Rankings

Match the letter of the sample to the ranking that fits it best.
Hint: Review the Elements of Fluency list in the first part of the lesson. Keep the list in mind as you rank the three samples for fluency.

_____ BEST IN FLUENCY: Top notch! Smooth, fluent, and varied.

_____ RUNNER-UP: Not bad, but a bit inconsistent.

_____ NEEDS WORK: A challenge—irregular stops and starts.

Revision Time

Select one of the samples that you rated as less than fluent.
How can you make it flow better? Refer to the Elements of
Fluency list. Mark the sample before you rewrite: cross out
words, vary beginnings, rewrite sentences, and add or replace
words and details. Then, use the writing space provided to
write your revised passage.

_____

_____

_____

_____

_____

_____

_____

A Writer's Question

Look again at the Elements of Fluency list.
Which of the items is one of your writing
strengths? Which item is one you still need
to work on?

Smooth Sailing

Whether piloting an airplane or an ocean-going ship, the captain is responsible for charting the smoothest course possible. A captain must do more than flick on the "Fasten Seatbelt!" sign or shout, "Batten down the hatches!" when the going gets rough. As a writer, you're captain of your ideas. You're in control of the text, and you need all of your skills when obstacles interrupt the fluency of your work. In this unit you've revised writing to increase fluency. You've practiced varying sentence beginnings to improve rhythm and heighten interest, and you've used transitions to connect ideas without overwhelming your readers. Now you'll put these skills together and revise a piece of your own writing.

Captain's Choice

Select a sample of your own writing that needs revision for sentence fluency. Look through your writing folder or journal, or select a project or report from science, math, or history. Remember, you're searching for a piece that needs better fluency. Be honest with yourself in selecting an appropriate example.

Teaming Up

To get the focused feedback you need, you'll work in small groups. Take turns sharing your writing aloud with your group. *Read your work just as it is*; don't make excuses or negative comments. Share, listen, and respond. The goal is to improve sentence fluency for everyone in your group.

As a Responder Focus your comments on fluency. Ask questions and make positive suggestions about strategies to improve sentence fluency. Remember, all comments should be supportive.

As a Writer Keep your eyes, ears, and mind open. Note helpful suggestions on your work. Incorporate useful comments and insights when you revise. Also, don't expect others to hear your writing exactly the way you do. Keep in mind that you want to make your writing better.

Charting a Course for Revision

After you've shared your writing sample and received some feedback, it's time for revision. Look over the strategies on pages 89 and 90, and put a check next to each one that might help your writing. **Tip:** Keep your group's comments and questions in mind as you select strategies. Also look at the notes you made and ask yourself, "Which strategies will help make my writing stronger and more fluent?"

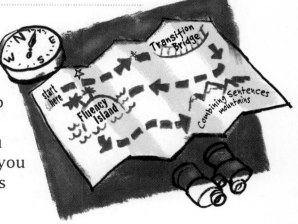

_____ Varying the beginnings of sentences.

_____ Selecting and placing transition/linking words to help ideas flow.

_____ Eliminating transition overload.

_____ Combining sentences. (Putting short, choppy sentences together to create a longer one.)

_____ Varying the length of sentences. (Counting the words in each sentence to check for variety.)

_____ Shortening over-long sentences and correcting run-ons.

_____ My own idea: _____

Write Now!

On a separate sheet of paper, revise the piece you selected. Focus on sentence fluency. Use the checklist of strategies you filled out, any notes you took with your group, and your student rubric for fluency. Take charge and make the changes you need to make!

Share and Compare

When you've finished revising, meet with one member of your sharing group. Take turns reading your revised work aloud. Be prepared to discuss the kinds of changes you made and the strategies you used. Give your partner specific, positive feedback. Your partner needs to hear what you liked about his or her revisions. Take in your partner's positive comments about your work, as well.

A Writer's Question

You won't always have a group or a partner to help you improve your writing. What can you do on your own to keep your writing fluent?

Unit 6
Conventions

Conventions are a matter of courtesy. Just as you help vacuum and dust to make guests comfortable in your home, you need to "tidy up" the conventions to make readers comfortable with your text. At the very least, this means checking your spelling, punctuation, and grammar. How important is this kind of courtesy? Well, most people would not dream of greeting a guest at the door and handing him or her a feather duster. Yet if you do not edit your work, you're saying to the reader, "Look here, I'm worn out with just writing this. I think I'll leave the editing to you." Some readers are such good sports that they don't mind dealing with a few errors. However, every error you leave in your text decreases the time and energy your reader can devote to thinking about your ideas, appreciating your voice, and enjoying your word choices and fluency.

In this unit, you'll learn about

◆ the difference between editing and revision

◆ spotting errors in faulty text

◆ recognizing and applying editing symbols

◆ creating a personal editing checklist

name: .... date: ....

straighten It Up

Let's say that your parents are expecting company. One of them asks you to straighten your room. You proceed to repaint your walls, replace your furniture, and lay new carpeting. "Whoa!" you may be thinking, "I wouldn't go that far. On a good day, I might dust or vacuum, if bribed sufficiently." Well—that would be "straightening" on a very different level, right? In writing, revising and editing are different ways of tidying up, too. Revising calls for sweeping changes, and editing adds the finishing touches. Both steps are essential to the writing process. If you perform these functions well, readers can concentrate on your ideas and appreciate your style.

Before and After: Notice the Difference?

The following passages will help you understand the difference between revising and editing. Read both samples carefully to determine whether the changes are examples of revising or of editing.

Sample 1

Before: We set up the tent in the yard. We camped in our yard. It was the last weekend before summer was over. The birds were noisy in the morning. We could hear everything. My friends and I slept in the tent. Our baseball team kept winning tournaments. We had a baseball tournament every weekend. We always camp in the summer. This wasn't real camping, but it wasn't bad. We could see stars.

After: It was the last weekend before school would start, and we hadn't been camping once. Usually my family takes several camping trips, and I get to bring along a couple of my friends. This summer, though, my friends and I were all on the same baseball team, going to tournament after tournament. The problem was, strange as it may sound, we kept winning—and all the camping time was slipping away until we were down to our last weekend. My dad is the one who came up with the idea to get out the tent and set it up in the corner of our yard. We jumped at the idea.

We got everything set up inside the tent, but we didn't go in until it was dark. We could hear every sound from the neighborhood: cars, crickets, people talking, dogs barking, and even two cats chasing each other along the fence. It was hard to fall asleep until we got used to the sounds. You could see some constellations through the mesh netting at the top of the tent; and when there weren't any cars going by, it seemed as though we were out in the woods. It wasn't real camping, but it was close enough.

What kinds of changes did the writer make?

_____

_____

_____

_____

Did the writer revise or edit? Explain your answer.

_____

_____

Sample 2

Before: we set up the the tent in the yard We was camped in are yard.
It was the the last weekend. Before summer was over. The birds noisey in the
morning. We coud hear everything. me and my freinds sleeped in the tent, our
baseball team kept winning turnamints. We had baseball turnamint every week
ends. We always camped in the summer. This isnt real camping. but it wasn't bad?
we could sea stars.

After: We set up the tent in the yard. We camped in our yard. It was the last
weekend before summer was over. The birds were noisy in the morning. We could
hear everything. My friends and I slept in the tent. Our baseball team kept winning
tournaments. We had a baseball tournament every weekend. We always camp in the
summer. This wasn't real camping, but it wasn't bad. We could see stars.

What kinds of changes did the writer make?

_____

_____

_____

_____

_____

Did the writer revise or edit? Explain your answer.

_____

_____

Share and Compare

Compare the changes you noted in the samples with those of a
partner. Decide whether the writer was revising or editing in
each sample. If you disagree with your partner, review the
reasons for your choice. You may change your mind, but only
if your partner has real evidence to convince you.

Narrowing It Down

Read each item carefully and decide whether it describes **revising** or **editing.** Then, circle your choice.

1. Combine three short sentences to make one longer sentence.

   Revising   **Editing**

2. Change "went" to "skipped rapidly across the wet pavement" to make the action clearer.

   Revising   **Editing**

3. Insert quotation marks around a character's dialogue.

   Revising   **Editing**

4. Delete two sentences that aren't connected to the main idea.

   Revising   **Editing**

Definitions

Now you will create your own definitions that tell what writers do when they revise and when they edit.

Revising is _____

_____ .

Editing is _____

_____ .

A Writer's Question

Revising and editing are two different activities. Does this mean that you can't do them simultaneously?

name: .... date: ....

Gliding Down the Highway

Striking ideas, original word choice, logical organization, strong voice, and fluid sentences may never get a reader's attention if they're surrounded by spelling, grammar, and punctuation errors. They're like beautiful scenery that goes unnoticed because the road is full of potholes. If you want your readers to glide along the highway of your ideas, you need to smooth the way by editing your work. A personalized checklist can help.

If I Were You

Reviewing the following writing sample will prepare you to review your own work. With a partner, identify and mark any problems you find. Then, prioritize them. Which are most significant? List five to ten items this writer should work on.

My sister is is always deiting, and it makes me crazy! Their is realy no reason for

to do this since she is as thin as a pencil right now I keep telling her that she is

thin enough to be a model but she just tells me what do you know." her name is heather and it is a good Name for her because she she is about as skinney as a twig if you ask me all this dieting people do is not that good of an idea heather mostly does it because when you are super skinney you can buy very tiny cloths on sale big deal (or maybe i should say small deal!

Personalized Checklist for This Writer:

1. _____
2. _____
3. _____
4. _____
5. _____
6. _____
7. _____
8. _____
9. _____
10. _____

Make a List

Select two or more pieces from your writing folder. Read them to identify the editing problems that appear most often. Look closely and be totally honest. Should you add punctuation? Do proper nouns lack capital letters? Is your paragraphing correct? Are any words doubled or missing? Do subjects and verbs agree? Place these and any other problems on your list on page 98. You need not fill every line, but be sure to list your main editing problems.

My Personalized Editing Checklist

Created by and for _____

1. _____

2. _____

3. _____

4. _____

5. _____

6. _____

7. _____

8. _____

9. _____

10. _____

Share and Compare

When your list is complete, meet with a partner to share your observations. (Your lists are personalized, so don't expect them to be identical.) As you share, look for similarities. Place a check mark next to any editing problems that appear on both lists. Is there anything on your partner's list that should appear on yours? If so, add it.

The Shrinking List

Keep a copy of your personalized editing checklist at home, in your notebook (for writing that comes up in your other classes) and in your writing folder. If you use your list as part of your writing routine, you'll notice that it will gradually shrink. Let's say that you have written three or four papers without making a particular error.

Cross that item off your list. Continue to be honest with yourself as you evaluate your writing, and your list will continue to shrink until it disappears!

Make a commitment right now: choose one editing problem from your list and underline it. You've just targeted that problem as the one you're going to work on for the next week or two. See whether you can eliminate this error from your list forever!

A Writer's Question

What is the first editing problem that you want to cross off your list? As a reader, what's the first thing that you'd like to cross off another writer's list?

Lesson 23

How Symbolic!

You know that a symbol stands for or represents something else. A flag, for example, can be a symbol for a country. Editors use symbols also. You may be familiar with and use editing symbols to put the final touches on your own writing or that of a classmate. When you use editing symbols to find and correct errors in conventions, you free readers to focus on your ideas.

Sixteen Symbols

This lesson provides a review of editing symbols you already know and an opportunity to learn a few more. Take time now to study the chart of editing symbols on the following page.

Editing Symbols

	Mark	Meaning	Use
1.	✎	Delete (Take it out.)	My dog is the my friend.
2.	∧	Add a word.	Pizza is ᵐʸ favorite food.
3.	≡	Capitalize this letter.	I live in portland.
4.	/	Make this a lowercase letter.	My sister is Older than I am.
5.	⊙	Add a period.	I am leaving on Tuesday⊙
6.	∧,	Add a comma.	I ate juice, toast, and cereal.
7.	⌄'	Add an apostrophe.	The neighbors dog bit me.
8.	⌄⌄' ⌄⌄'	Add quotation marks.	I'm having a blast, he shouted.
9.	¶	Start a new paragraph.	"Wild dogs!" yelled Joe. ¶ "Should we run?" Jacob asked.
10.	(Run in)	No new paragraph; sentences should run together.	Skateboarding is more fun (Run in) than walking. It's even more fun than flying.
11.	∧	Change a letter or word.	I'm done with the yard.
12.	∪	Transpose the order of letters or words.	It was a dark night.
13.	⌃?	Add a question mark.	Do you want to go?
14.	‿	Close up.	Pa per or plastic?
15.	stet	Put deleted material back in.	Would you like ˢᵗᵉᵗ paper or plastic?
16.	⌃#	Insert space.	Here comes Jane.

Warming Up with Symbols

Think of symbols as instant messaging between writer and editor. In these two warm-up exercises, the editor has left coded instant messages for the writer. Write the messages that these symbols send.

1. "when are going to be there" whined Kevin from the back

   seat. "im really tired and I have to go to the bathroom.

Instant Message to the Writer: The writer needs to _____

_____

_____ .

2. Are poor tomato plants looked as though they were about to

   die We Had only been gone Three days (but It had bean

   over 100 degrease each day)

Instant Message to the Writer: The writer needs to _____

_____

_____ .

Share and Compare

Share your instant message translations with a partner. Could both of you "read" the editor's messages? Were your translations similar?

Editing with Symbols

Here's a writing sample that needs editing. As you read, use editing symbols to tell the writer how to polish the work. For this exercise, focus on putting in the symbols; don't correct the errors. If necessary, refer to the Editing Symbols chart.

Saturday, Septe

4:00 PM t

Metacomet C
500 Veterans Me
East Provi

$30.00 pe

Tickets Available throu
East Providence High
Central Administration
Mary Shadrick (438-0816) or

Hors d'Ouevres   Pasta

Traffic Jam Destiny

I dont kn ow what it is about my mom but she has alot of bad luck as a driver. Let me give you a few examples of here bad luck. To get to my drum teachers house we have togo dwon a vary busy street, the kind that has a traffic light every block. Whenever were running a few minutes late, her bad luck kicks in and we become a red light magnt I swear that some lights see use coming swtich from green to red with out (even a bit of) yellow in between. We always seem to find every road that is under Construction as well. Roads that just moments before were probably free and clear spot, us moving twoard them and instantly jam up with orange cones and large excavating equipment. On top of all this, my mom attract s every train slow moving vehicle out their. Eventually we always get where were gooing.

A Writer's Question

In addition to the short instant messages you sent to the writer in the last exercise, what message could you send to help the writer understand the connection between ideas and conventions?

name: .... date: ....

The Editing
Express Lane

A smart grocery shopper who selects only the necessary
items may be able to check out in the Express Lane.
Editing is a little like that. Sometimes all the writing needs
is polish—ten items or fewer. Then it's ready for the
Editing Express Lane. But other pieces come with
a cartload of errors, making checkout slow. This lesson
will prepare you for Express Lane checkout. You've been
working on the skills you need: focused eyes and ears to
see and hear errors, an understanding of the basic rules
of language, and knowledge of editor's symbols. Practice
these for a while, and you'll soon move confidently into
the Editing Express Lane.

Warming Up to the Job

The secret to good editing is practice. Read the following
passage aloud softly, looking and listening for errors. Use the
editing symbols from the chart in Lesson 23 to mark errors,
but do not correct them. If you aren't sure which symbol to
use, circle the item for now. Then count the total number
of errors.

Moving From one city to another is hard but whne the new city in a different state as well, moving can make it even harder. My mom recently got an important job promotion. To get the promotion we had to move from Eagle, Idaho, to Rockwall, texas. Before we made the big move, we flew to Texas to get feel for our new twon and to look for a house

It turns out that Eagel and Rockwall aren't totally different. Eagle is close to Boise, a large city; and Rockwall is close to Dallas, and even big ger city. But thats about as close as they some to being similar. Eagle has Mountains that are close buy; you can see them from my old house. Rockwall has a water tower that you can sea from the drive way of the house my mom liked. You no how it is nothing compares to what your used to It will be OK as soon as Learn to speak Texan.

My Review

Number of errors I spotted: _____

Number of different editing symbols I used: _____

I would say that this writing is

_____ ready for the Editing Express Lane.

_____ almost ready—just an item or two over.

_____ nowhere close—this cart is overloaded!

Getting Better

Use the appropriate editing symbols to mark errors in this passage, too.

my parents alsways told me that the the reason they liked to travel so muych was because every where they went they learned something about their own lives by learning about how other People lived. of cours e, this was also the reason they took us on soo many trips with them   I dont know if I always learned new things aobut my life, but I did see alot of amazing and sometimes, strange things. about a year ago, we were driving through some of the states that didn't have any Pins in them   my dad liked to place pins with little flags on this map to show all the places we've been.

North Dakota was one of the states without any pins. nothing against north Dakota, but it's not exactly the place vacationers think of When they plan a trip.

All I really knew about North Dakota wa sthat it often had the coldest winter Temperatures. in the United States and that it was above South DAkota. we where driving threw the middle of nowhere when we came upon this little town this little town right around dinner time. There were only two restaurants one was a coffee shop and the other was an italian place, my dad's choice. We all kind of laughed at the idea of finding an Italina restaurant in this little town in north Dakota the man who led us to our table said, "Welcome to Napolitano's, a little slice of Italy just for you then he shouted something in Italian to another man who had poked his head out of the kitchen door.

I knew this was the kind of place my parents would love.

My Review

Number of errors I spotted: _____

Number of different editing symbols I used: _____

I would say that this writing is

_____ ready for the Editing Express Lane.

_____ almost ready—just an item or two over.

_____ nowhere close—this cart is overloaded!

A Writer's Question

Do errors occur because the writer lacks skill in the trait of conventions or because the writer works too fast and fails to pay enough attention? Which explanation applies to your errors? What does this tell you about how to improve your editing?

Wrap-up Activity 1

Tips & Speed Bumps

Your job is to explain the traits so clearly that a writer will know just what to do and what to avoid. To do this, you need to come up with two "Tips for Success" and two "Speed Bumps" (things that get in the way of success) for each of the six traits. For example, for the trait of conventions, one tip for success might be to check spelling more than once. One "speed bump" might be forgetting to insert punctuation.

Tips for IDEAS

1. _____

2. _____

Speed Bumps

1. _____

2. _____

Tips for ORGANIZATION

1. _____

2. _____

Speed Bumps

1. _____

2. _____

Tips for VOICE

1. _____

2. _____

Speed Bumps

1. _____

2. _____

Tips for WORD CHOICE

1. _____

2. _____

Speed Bumps

1. _____

2. _____

Tips for SENTENCE FLUENCY

1. _____

2. _____

Speed Bumps

1. _____

2. _____

Tips for CONVENTIONS

1. _____

2. _____

Speed Bumps

1. _____

2. _____

Wrap-up Activity 2

Spotting a Problem

Each of the following writing samples has a major problem with one of the traits. Read each passage carefully to identify the trait.

Sample 1

We should have a leash law. Without a leash law, dogs run wild. Sometimes they chase people on bikes. Sometimes they wreck people's gardens. Dogs occasionally chase joggers. We really need a leash law.

The MAIN problem with this paragraph is _____

because _____ .

Sample 2

The scariest thing that ever happened to me was being stuck on a roller coaster. We were stuck upside down for about four hours while some workers tried to fix it. It was just extremely scary. We could hear them working on it the whole time. You would think when you're up that high, you could really see for a long way. However, when you are upside down, it's much harder to know what you are looking at. We were all relieved to get back on the ground. I felt tired and extremely thirsty after this experience. It really was scary.

The MAIN problem with this paragraph is _____

because _____ .

Sample 3

Last week, a special visitor came to our local bookstore. She was a famous author from the northwestern United States who has written about five or six books, some for adults and some for other ages. During her author visits, she reads from her books and then gives the audience an opportunity to ask questions. Though you might have read one of her books, it is very exciting to see an author in person and to hear her read her own work. It was great.

The MAIN problem with this paragraph is _____

because _____ .

Sample 4

It might seem that igniting fires is an odd way to control fire outbreaks. Of course, this controlled burning needs to happen before fire season. What happens over time is that the undergrowth in forests—the bushes and small plants—gets out of hand. Normally rain is helpful in keeping fire danger minimal, but if it produces too much undergrowth, rain can actually aggravate the problem, even though that seems ironic. Anyway, sometimes the forest service decides to burn the undergrowth to reduce the forest fire hazard. Of course, if a fire does break out, forest rangers hope for more rain. Otherwise, they might need to start a controlled burn.

The MAIN problem with this paragraph is _____

because _____ .

Wrap-up Activity 3

Making a Diagnosis

This time, you will analyze a piece of writing for strengths and problems across all six traits. Use the rubrics to mark the scores you would give "The Storyteller" for each trait.

The Storyteller

Whenever I visited my grandmother's house, we we would sit down together to tell stories. She let me drink coffee even though I was only ten or eleven at the time (I forget my exact age).

My favorite stories were always about her cat Rufus. He was a fighter. In fact, Rufus would even fight with dogs sometimes—and win!

One time my grandmother told me a story about killing a rattlesnake. I drank two cups of coffee during that story! It seems she was a teacher in a one-room schoolhouse out on the prairie some where. She had to drive a team of horses to school. This is hard to imagine now with highways everywhere and everyone (just about) owning a car. Anyway, when she pulled her team up to the school and got out, she saw something by the door. At first, she though it was a scarf dropped by one of her students. When she got closer, she saw that it was moving! The "scarf" came to life! It was a four-foot rattlesnake. Quick as lightning, my grandmother grabed the rake she kept by the school door and hit the rattler with it. This was a dangerous thing to do because the snake could have bitten her; but luckily, she stunned it. Then she killed it. She told a lot of other stories at different times when I visited her but that one has remained my favorite to this day.

IDEAS

_____ 1 _____ 2 _____ 3 _____ 4 _____ 5 _____ 6

ORGANIZATION

_____ 1 _____ 2 _____ 3 _____ 4 _____ 5 _____ 6

VOICE

_____ 1 _____ 2 _____ 3 _____ 4 _____ 5 _____ 6

WORD CHOICE

_____ 1 _____ 2 _____ 3 _____ 4 _____ 5 _____ 6

SENTENCE FLUENCY

_____ 1 _____ 2 _____ 3 _____ 4 _____ 5 _____ 6

CONVENTIONS

_____ 1 _____ 2 _____ 3 _____ 4 _____ 5 _____ 6